Language Is Sermonic

Language Is Sermonic

*Richard M. Weaver
on the Nature of Rhetoric*

Edited by

RICHARD L. JOHANNESEN
RENNARD STRICKLAND
RALPH T. EUBANKS

LOUISIANA STATE UNIVERSITY PRESS

BATON ROUGE AND LONDON

1970

Acknowledgment is made for permission to reprint Professor Weaver's essays: "The *Phaedrus* and the Nature of Rhetoric" and "Ultimate Terms in Contemporary Rhetoric," both in Weaver, *The Ethics of Rhetoric* (Chicago: Henry Regnery, 1953); "The Power of the Word," in Weaver, *Ideas Have Consequences* (Chicago: University of Chicago Press, 1948); "Relativism and the Use of Language," in Helmut Schoeck and James W. Wiggins (eds.), *Relativism and the Study of Man* (New York: Van Nostrand, 1961) copyright © 1961 by William Volker Fund; "Concealed Rhetoric in Scientistic Sociology," in *Georgia Review*, XIII (Spring, 1959); "The Cultural Role of Rhetoric," in Weaver, *Visions of Order* (Baton Rouge: Louisiana State University Press, 1964); "To Write the Truth," in *College English*, X (October, 1948); and "Language Is Sermonic," in Roger E. Nebergall (ed.), *Dimensions of Rhetorical Scholarship* (Norman: University of Oklahoma Department of Speech, 1963).

Acknowledgment is also made for permission to reprint "Richard M. Weaver, Friend of Traditional Rhetoric: An Appreciation," which originally appeared, in somewhat different form, as "Richard M. Weaver: In Memoriam," in *Georgia Review*, XVII (Winter, 1963).

Library Of Congress Catalog Card Number 73-119114
ISBN 0-8071-0424-8 (cloth); ISBN 0-8071-1221-6 (paper)

Designed by Jules B. McKee

Louisiana Paperback Edition, 1985

Contents

Richard M. Weaver, Friend of Traditional Rhetoric:
AN APPRECIATION   by Ralph T. Eubanks ... 3

Richard M. Weaver on the Nature of Rhetoric:
AN INTERPRETATION   by Richard L. Johannesen,
Rennard Strickland, and Ralph T. Eubanks ... 7

The Power of the Word ... 33

The Phaedrus and the Nature of Rhetoric ... 57

Ultimate Terms in Contemporary Rhetoric ... 87

Relativism and the Use of Language ... 115

Concealed Rhetoric in Scientistic Sociology ... 139

The Cultural Role of Rhetoric ... 161

To Write the Truth ... 187

Language Is Sermonic ... 201

Index ... 227

Language Is Sermonic

*[T]he embattled friends of traditional rhetoric
. . . are in my opinion the upholders of our
inherited society.*

—Richard M. Weaver to Ralph T. Eubanks
September 2, 1959

Richard M. Weaver,
Friend of Traditional Rhetoric:
AN APPRECIATION

by Ralph T. Eubanks

RICHARD M. WEAVER was one of those rare souls who
had thought deeply about what he was doing. He had
settled for himself a vast number of things about the meaning of his life and the world. And he was therefore left free
to follow his "duty and destiny" in the Carlylian sense.
Weaver, a professor of humanities, became ultimately what
he called a "doctor of culture." He believed, and passion-
ately so, that the inherited traditions of our society were in
process of rapid disintegration. And Reinhold Niebuhr regarded his seminal analysis *Ideas Have Consequences* as "a
profound diagnosis of the sickness of our culture."

The heart of Weaver's mission was restoration of respect
for what T. S. Eliot once called "the permanent things."
The final sanction of his case was intuitive. "We begin our

other affirmations," he wrote, "after a categorical statement that life and the world are to be cherished." Thus it was that Weaver was inevitably thrust into opposition to the Jacobin mentality.

In the fulfillment of his duty and destiny he became the man he described in a letter to the writer—one of "the embattled friends of traditional rhetoric." In Weaver's judgment these men were "the upholders of our inherited society." That is, they were the prime conservators of the values essential to cultural cohesion.

Thus, in a very real sense Weaver's life was a crusade to reestablish belief in the reality of transcendentals. "For four centuries," he observed in *Ideas Have Consequences*, "every man has been not only his own priest but his own professor of ethics, and the consequence is an anarchy which threatens even that minimum consensus of value necessary to the political state."

Richard Weaver fully understood the magnitude of his task. And his mission became for him in his later years an almost consuming passion. At Christmas, 1962, I received from him a simple greeting card which says much about the nature of his commitment. Scribbled beneath the printed greeting was a postscript—a kind of afterthought: "There is much to be done."

Weaver was always aware that his cause required the strongest of rhetorical strategies. He settled upon John Crowe Ransom's notion of "the unorthodox defense of orthodoxy" and he followed that rhetorical design to the end of his career.

His defense of orthodoxy began and ended with the southern idea of life. Weaver was a man of the South. Yet, true to his conception of the rhetor-as-cultural-critic, he exiled himself from his native South. His most mature thought was really the product of his years at the University of Chicago—years in a climate he found so hostile that he often wore two overcoats. Ironically, only a few months before his death Weaver had accepted an appointment at Vanderbilt in his beloved South.

Weaver's first article, "The Older Religiousness in the South," dealt with the South's intense religiosity; one of his very last, "The Southern Phoenix," was a review of Harper's reissue of *I'll Take My Stand*; his latest posthumous book is *The Southern Tradition at Bay*. In the intervening years he conducted a memorable defense of those orthodoxies centering in Christianity, political conservatism, and Ciceronian humanism. His searching analyses took the measure of modern nihilism in all its guises.

Weaver's "unorthodox defense" began with an awareness that orthodoxy was in retreat "owing to a kind of default." The defense he made was a manly one. He gained the necessary knowledge, then argued his case with boldness and cogency. He spoke in a disarming modern idiom, and avoided all "mawkish apology." As Russell Kirk has observed, Weaver was "no pretentious moralizer." Rather, he was—to use one of his own terms—"an honest seeker."

Weaver's rhetoric drew power from his "passion for the actual." He understood—in Emerson's phrase—that "the scholar loses no hour which the man lives." And he was acutely aware of the danger in letting one's dialectic get separated from the real world. Though he was a bachelor who lived apart much of the time, he was not a recluse. He enjoyed the Kaffeeklatsche with its opportunity to be—as he liked to put it—"a practicing humanist"; the yearly Christmas sojourn at his ancestral home in North Carolina where he could engage in pleasant reminiscences with relatives and come into contact again with the mystery of

nature; and the occasional sally into the world of the sports-
man where he worked as hard at rifle marksmanship as he
did at the polishing of an essay in the privacy of his rented
apartment.

In Richard Weaver's life and work is the stubborn testimony of the spiritual in man. His writings speak with
promise to the unsatisfied poetic and ethical hungers of our
times. And they show with impressive clarity how the
hard-won wisdom of man's past may be effectively defended. They do more. They inspire faith that the moral,
aesthetic, and religious realms of human experience will
endure. In his essay "The Southern Phoenix," which appeared about the time of his death, he wrote: "It is possible
to affirm a humane order in the face of the most towering
odds, and by faith and work it is possible to achieve it."
The "humane order" Weaver envisioned was an order ani-
mated by the ancient virtue of *piety* and premised upon a
proper partnership between sentiment and reason, between
rhetoric and dialectic.

The art of rhetoric itself was for Weaver a crucial part
of the orthodoxy he sought by his own rhetoric to reani-
mate. Indeed, the renewal of this ancient art seemed to
him the first order of business in a world with blurred
moral vision. He labored tirelessly to find out the "true
nature" of rhetoric, locating its taproot at last in an essential property of man's being—the power to conceive
value. And he strove with all the rhetorical skill at his command to convey to the modern mind his vision of the right
use of rhetoric. "His greatest achievement," Wilma Ebbitt
has correctly observed, "was to build a coherent body of
rhetorical principles that have validity *here and now*"
(italics mine).

Richard M. Weaver
on the Nature of Rhetoric:
AN INTERPRETATION

by Richard L. Johannesen, Rennard Strickland,
and Ralph T. Eubanks

MODERN PHILOSOPHER Eliseo Vivas uses the ancient term "rhetor" to describe the late Richard M. Weaver. Vivas contends that Weaver saw the importance of rhetoric, in its classical sense, as "no other thinker among us . . . has seen it."[1] Weaver remains, no doubt, one of the most stimulating and controversial rhetorical theorists of our time. From the outset of his career he has provided, as Paul Tillich observes of his first work, "philosophical shock—the beginning of wisdom." Over the years, Weaver's views on the nature of rhetoric have had increasing influence among rhetorical scholars.[2]

---

[1] Eliseo Vivas, "The Mind of Richard Weaver," *Modern Age*, VIII (Summer, 1964), 309; Vivas, "Introduction," in Weaver, *Life Without Prejudice and Other Essays* (Chicago: Regnery, 1965), xiii–xiv. When Weaver died at age fifty-three, April 3, 1963, he was professor of English in the College of the University of Chicago.

[2] For the influence of Weaver's ideas on other rhetorical theorists see Maurice Natanson, "The Limits of Rhetoric," *Quarterly Journal of Speech*,

Weaver as a social critic has sought to clarify the role of rhetoric in improving a declining modern culture. At one point in *Visions of Order* he described a "kind of doctor of culture," a description which could also serve as a virtual self-portrait of his own function. Even though a member of the culture, this "doctor" in some degree had estranged himself from his culture through study and reflection. He had "acquired knowledge and developed habits of thought which enable him to see it in perspective and to gauge it."[3]

Although he wrote a large number of articles, essays, lectures, books, and book reviews both on academic and political subjects,[4] Weaver's views on rhetoric can be

XLI (April, 1955), 133–39; Virgil Baker and Ralph Eubanks, *Speech in Personal and Public Affairs* (New York: David McKay, 1965), viii, 74, 80, 113; Ralph Eubanks and Virgil Baker, "Toward an Axiology of Rhetoric," *Quarterly Journal of Speech*, XLVIII (April, 1962), 157–68; Walter R. Fisher, "Advisory Rhetoric: Implications for Forensic Debate," *Western Speech*, XXIX (Spring, 1965), 114–19; Donald Davidson, "Grammar and Rhetoric: The Teacher's Problem," *Quarterly Journal of Speech*, XXXIX (December, 1953), 424–36; Ralph T. Eubanks, "Nihilism and the Problem of a Worthy Rhetoric," *Southern Speech Journal*, XXXIII (Spring, 1968), 187–99; W. Ross Winterowd, *Rhetoric: A Synthesis* (New York: Holt, Rinehart and Winston, 1968), 9–10, 13. Some of Weaver's essays now are being reprinted in anthologies on rhetoric. See, for example, Joseph Schwartz and John Rycenga (eds.), *The Province of Rhetoric* (New York: Ronald Press, 1965), 275–92, 311–29; Dudley Bailey (ed.), *Essays on Rhetoric* (New York: Oxford University Press, 1965), 234–49; Maurice Natanson and Henry W. Johnstone (eds.), *Philosophy, Rhetoric, and Argumentation* (University Park: Pennsylvania State University Press, 1965), 63–79.

[3] Although most of his writings on rhetoric have this thrust, one of his most clearly focused essays was "The Cultural Role of Rhetoric," in *Visions of Order* (Baton Rouge: Louisiana State University Press, 1964), Chap. 4. See also page 7.

[4] The editors wish to acknowledge the cooperation of Louis Dehmlow, compiler of Weaver's papers, and the late Kendall Beaton, literary executor, in securing a bibliography of Weaver's writings and copies of some of Weaver's unpublished manuscripts. A complete bibliography of Weaver's published writings appears in his *The Southern Tradition at Bay*, edited by George Core and M. E. Bradford (New York: Arlington House, 1968), 401–18.

gleaned primarily from the following published sources: *Ideas Have Consequences*, a post-World War II critique of American society; *The Ethics of Rhetoric*; *Composition*, a college textbook; "Language is Sermonic," a lecture delivered to a graduate speech seminar at the University of Oklahoma; *Visions of Order*, a posthumously published critique of our present society; *Life Without Prejudice and Other Essays*, a collection of previously published essays; "Relativism and the Use of Language"; "Concealed Rhetoric in Scientistic Sociology"; and "To Write the Truth."[5]

Weaver held two basic orientations that are of prime importance to an understanding of his rhetorical views.[6] First, politically he was a conservative of some note. Leading conservatives such as Russell Kirk and Willmoore Kendall held him in esteem.[7] Weaver was, for example, an associate editor of the conservative *Modern Age*, a contributor to *National Review*, a trustee of the Intercollegiate Society of Individualists, and a recipient in 1962 of a na-

[5] *Ideas Have Consequences* (Chicago: University of Chicago Press, 1948); *The Ethics of Rhetoric* (Chicago: Regnery, 1953); *Composition: A Course in Writing and Rhetoric* (New York: Holt, Rinehart and Winston, 1957); "Language Is Sermonic," in Roger E. Nebergall (ed.), *Dimensions of Rhetorical Scholarship* (Norman: University of Oklahoma Department of Speech, 1963); *Visions of Order*; *Life Without Prejudice and Other Essays*; "Relativism and the Use of Language," in H. Schoeck and J. W. Wiggins (eds.), *Relativism and the Study of Man* (New York: Van Nostrand, 1961), 236–54; "Concealed Rhetoric in Scientistic Sociology," *Georgia Review*, XIII (Spring, 1959), 19–32; "To Write the Truth," *College English*, X (October, 1948), 25–30.

[6] James Powell, "The Foundations of Weaver's Traditionalism," *New Individualist Review*, III (1964), 3–7; E. Victor Milione, "The Uniqueness of Richard M. Weaver," *Intercollegiate Review*, II (September, 1965), 67.

[7] Russell Kirk, "Richard Weaver, R I P," *National Review*, XIV (April 23, 1963), 308; Willmoore Kendall, "How to Read Richard Weaver," *Intercollegiate Review*, II (September, 1965), 77–86. In fact Kendall argues that Weaver was so unique that he was virtually the only true American conservative on the contemporary scene.

tional award from the Young Americans for Freedom. In his public lectures, such as "How to Argue the Conservative Cause," he actively advocated rational conservatism.

In his mid-twenties Weaver had moved from arch-socialist to ardent conservative.[8] A product of southern upbringing and education in North Carolina, Kentucky, Tennessee, and Louisiana, he defended Southern Agrarian traditions.[9] At Vanderbilt University he was exposed to the Southern Agrarian ideas of John Crowe Ransom, Robert Penn Warren, Donald Davidson, and Allen Tate.[10] Kendall contends that Weaver was more a commentator *on* Southern Agrarianism than a devotee of its ideals.[11] Weaver himself admitted that at Vanderbilt he felt a "powerful pull" toward the Agrarian ideals of the individual in contact with nature, the necessity of the small-property-hold-

[8] Weaver discusses this transition in his autobiographical article "Up from Liberalism," *Modern Age*, III (Winter, 1958–59), 21–32. Starting in 1932 he was a formal member of the American Socialist Party for at least two years.

[9] Weaver, "The Southern Tradition," *New Individualist Review*, III (1964), 7–17. Born in Asheville, North Carolina, in 1910, he received his B.A. from the University of Kentucky in 1932, M.A. from Vanderbilt University in 1934, and Ph.D. from Louisiana State University in 1943.

[10] For statements of Southern Agrarian precepts, including those of Ransom, Warren, Davidson, and Tate, see *I'll Take My Stand: The South and the Agrarian Tradition*, by Twelve Southerners (New York: Harper, 1930); see also Herbert Agar and Allen Tate, *Who Owns America? A New Declaration of Independence* (Boston: Houghton Mifflin, 1936). Ransom, Warren, Davidson, and Tate, who led the influential literary group known as the "Nashville Fugitives," reflect on their participation in the Southern Agrarian movement in Rob Roy Purdy (ed.), *Fugitives' Reunion: Conversations at Vanderbilt* (Nashville: Vanderbilt University Press, 1959), 177–218. Ransom directed Weaver's M.A. thesis on "The Revolt Against Humanism." A recent analysis of the Southern Agrarian philosophy is Alexander Karanikas, *Tillers of a Myth: Southern Agrarians as Social and Literary Critics* (Madison: University of Wisconsin Press, 1966).

[11] Kendall, "How to Read Richard Weaver," 78.

ing class, and a pluralistic society.[12] He left Vanderbilt poised between the opposites of socialism and Southern Agrarianism and by the early 1940's had firmly opted for conservatism generally and some particular facets of Southern Agrarianism.[13] For example, Weaver championed the Agrarian ideal of individual ownership of private property and disdain of science as inadequate to deal with values.[14] He desired in society law, order, and cohesive diversity. The just and ideal society, he believed, must reflect real hierarchy and essential distinctions. An orderly society following the vision of a Good Purpose, with men harmoniously functioning in their proper stations in the structure, constituted Weaver's goal.[15]

Secondly, Weaver was a devoted Platonic idealist.[16] Belief in the reality of transcendentals, the primacy of ideas, and the view that form is prior to substance constituted his philosophical foundation.[17] While not a Platonist in all matters, he yet looked for societal and personal salvation to ideals, essences, and principles rather than to the transitory, the changing, and the expedient. His view was antipragmatic and antiutilitarian. While general semanticist S. I.

[12] "Up from Liberalism," 23; Weaver, "The Confederate South, 1865–1910: A Study in the Survival of a Mind and Culture" (Ph.D. dissertation, Louisiana State University, 1943), 517. In a slightly revised form this dissertation has been published as *The Southern Tradition at Bay*.

[13] "Up from Liberalism," 23–24; Weaver, "The Tennessee Agrarians," *Shenandoah*, III (Summer, 1952), 3–10.

[14] *Who Owns America?*, 182–83, 325–26; *Ideas Have Consequences*, Chap. 7.

[15] *Ideas Have Consequences*, 20, 35–51, 74–75; *Visions of Order*, 13, 22–39.

[16] *Ideas Have Consequences*, 3–5, 12–17, 22–23, 34, 52, 60, 73, 119, 130–32, 146–47, 154; *Visions of Order*, 20–21, 38, 134–35; "Language Is Sermonic," 55; *Ethics of Rhetoric*, 3–26.

[17] Weaver, Foreword to *Ideas Have Consequences* (paperback, 1959), v; Weaver, *New York Times Book Review* (March 21, 1948), 29.

Hayakawa attacks Weaver's Platonic idealism, Russell Kirk praises Weaver as a "powerful mind given to meditation upon universals."[18]

The ultimate "goods" in society were of central concern to Weaver.[19] Reality for him was a hierarchy in which the ultimate Idea of the Good constituted the value standard by which all other existents could be appraised for degree of goodness and truth. Truth to him was the degree to which things and ideas in the material world conform to their ideals, archetypes, and essences. He contended that "the thing is not true and the act is not just unless these conform to a conceptual ideal."[20] What *the* ultimate Good was and how it is known through intuition, Weaver never really made clear. What comprised *his* ultimate Good was likewise unclear. But he viewed freedom, justice, and order as ideals toward which men and cultures must strive. The reality of nature he saw as a dualistic paradox of essences and transformations. "Whatever the field we gaze upon," he observed, "we see things maintaining their identity while changing. Things both *are* and *are becoming*. They are because the idea or general configuration of them persists; and they are becoming because with the flowing of time, they inevitably slough off old substance and take on new."[21]

Weaver held a complex conception of the nature of

[18] S. I. Hayakawa, *Symbol, Status, and Personality* (New York: Harcourt, Brace, and World, 1963), 154–70, 182–85; Russell Kirk, "Ethical Labors," *Sewanee Review*, LXII (July–Sept., 1954), 489.

[19] *Ideas Have Consequences*, 17, 51–52; *Ethics of Rhetoric*, 211–32.

[20] *Ideas Have Consequences*, 130, 4. For many of the insights in the following paragraphs concerning Weaver's philosophy of reality and knowledge, the authors wish to acknowledge the research of Thomas D. Clark. See Thomas D. Clark, "The Philosophical Bases of Richard M. Weaver's View of Rhetoric" (M.A. thesis, Indiana University, 1969).

[21] *Visions of Order*, 23.

knowledge. He partially agreed with Mortimer Adler that there are three "orders" of knowledge. First is the level of particulars and individual facts, the simple data of science. Second is the level of theories, propositions, and generalizations about these facts. Third is the level of philosophic evaluations and value judgments about such theories.[22] At this third level, Ideas, universals, and first principles function as judgmental standards. Knowledge based on particulars alone and on raw physical sensations is suspect since it is incomplete knowledge. True knowledge is of universals and first principles. Weaver adopted at one point the absolute position that "there is no knowledge at the level of sensation, and that therefore knowledge is of universals. . . . the fewer particulars we require in order to arrive at our generalization, the more apt pupils we are in the school of wisdom."[23] In two other books he suggested that Knowledge of universals comes through dialectic, the ability to differentiate existents into categories, and through intuition, the ability to grasp "essential correspondences."[24]

Weaver believed man's essential nature encompasses fixed elements, yet for him the good man seemed more an ideal than an actuality. He held that man's fundamental humanness is founded in four faculties, capacities, or modes of apprehension.[25] Man possesses a rational or cognitive capacity which gives him knowledge; an emotional or aesthetic capacity which allows him to experience pleasure, pain, and beauty; an ethical capacity which determines orders of goods and judges between right and wrong; and a religious capacity which provides yearning for something

[22] *Ethics of Rhetoric,* 30–31; *Ideas Have Consequences,* 18.
[23] *Ideas Have Consequences,* 12–13, 3, 27.
[24] *Visions of Order,* 12; *Ethics of Rhetoric,* 49–54, 56–57, 203–204.
[25] *Visions of Order,* 85; "Language Is Sermonic," 50–51; *Life Without Prejudice,* 146.

infinite and gives man a glimpse of his destiny and ultimate nature.

Weaver used a tripartite division of body, mind, and soul to further explain man's essential nature. The body, man's physical being, houses the mind and soul during life but extracts its due through a constant downward pull toward indiscriminate and excessive satisfaction of sensory pleasure. The body is self-centered and disdainful of worthy goals.[26] Man's mind or intellect provides him with the potential to apprehend the structure of reality, define concepts, and rationally order ideas. While giving man the capacity for knowledge and order, the mind is guided toward good or evil by the disposition of the soul.[27] Man's soul or spirit—depending upon whether it has been trained well or ill—guides the mind and body toward love of the good or toward love of physical pleasure. Weaver found the concept of soul difficult to explain; it seemed for him to encompass man's ethical and religious capacities.[28] The elements of man's essential nature he viewed as fixed. Yet he implied that the dominance of one component over others is determined by man's training, environment, and culture.

Weaver underscored two additional concepts in his analysis of man's uniquely human characteristics.[29] Man's capacity for choice-making affords him his dignity—if judiciously exercised in selecting means and ends. And as the

[26] *Visions of Order,* 9, 144; *Life Without Prejudice,* 146; *Ideas Have Consequences,* 18.

[27] *Visions of Order,* 24, 50, 85; *Ideas Have Consequences,* 19–20; *Life Without Prejudice,* 45–46.

[28] *Visions of Order,* 43–44, 47, 85, 144; *Ideas Have Consequences,* 19–20; *Ethics of Rhetoric,* 17, 23.

[29] *Visions of Order,* 135; *Ideas Have Consequences,* 167; *Life Without Prejudice,* 46–47. For Kenneth Burke's analysis of man as the symbol-using animal, see Burke, *Language as Symbolic Action* (Berkeley: University of California Press, 1966), 3–24.

symbol-using animal—although the definition is a partial one—man rises above the sensate and can communicate knowledge, feeling, and values.

In readily accepting the label of conservative, Weaver emphasized that a conservative believes there is a structure of reality independent of his own will and desire and accepts some principles as given, lasting, and good.[30] The true conservative for Weaver was one "who sees the universe as a paradigm of essences, of which the phenomenology of the world is a sort of continuing approximation. Or, to put it another way, he sees it as a set of definitions which are struggling to get themselves defined in the real world."[31]

These two fundamental orientations, political conservatism and Platonic idealism, led Weaver in *Ideas Have Consequences* and *Visions of Order* to indict contemporary Western culture for having lost faith in an order of "goods." Among the societal weaknesses and vices he condemned were the following: scientism, nominalism, semantic positivism, doctrinaire democracy, uncritical homage to the theory of evolution, radical egalitarianism, pragmatism, cultural relativism, materialism, emphasis on techniques at the expense of goals, idolization of youth, progressive education, disparagement of historical consciousness, deleterious effects of the mass media, and degenerate literature, music, and art.

Weaver outlined the program he thought necessary for the restoration of health to Western culture. Among his positive suggestions were the development of a sense of history; balance between permanence and change; reestablishment of faith in ideas, ideals, and principles; maintenance of the "metaphysical right" of private property; edu-

---

[30] *Life Without Prejudice*, 157–59.
[31] *Ethics of Rhetoric*, 112.

cation in literature, rhetoric, logic, and dialectic; respect for nature, the individual, and the ideals of the past; reemphasis on traditional education; and control (but not elimination) of war.[32]

From this vantage point Weaver expounded his view of the nature, function, and scope of rhetoric. As his writings on rhetoric show, he was familiar with the ancient theories of Plato, Aristotle, Cicero, and Quintilian.[33] And Plato's views on the subject held a special attraction for him. The influence of Kenneth Burke is also clearly reflected in Weaver's writings on rhetoric.[34] At one point Weaver views rhetoric as a process of making identifications and he widens the scope of rhetoric beyond linguistic forms to include a rhetoric of "matter or scene," as in the instance of a bank's erecting an imposing office building to strengthen its image.[35]

In Weaver's view, rhetoric makes convictions compelling by showing them in the contexts of reality and human values. Rhetoric, he wrote, is "persuasive speech in the service of truth"; it should "create an informed appetition for the good."[36] It affects us "primarily by setting forth images which inform and attract." And generally, rhetoric

[32] Some of Weaver's positive suggestions were propounded in *Ideas Have Consequences* and *Visions of Order*; others were presented in some of his articles such as "The Humanities in a Century of Common Man," *New Individualist Review*, III (1964), 17–24. See also *Life Without Prejudice*, 15–64, 99–120; *The Southern Tradition at Bay*, 29–44, 388–96.

[33] Wilma R. Ebbitt, "Richard M. Weaver, Teacher of Rhetoric," *Georgia Review*, XVIII (Winter, 1963), 417. These ancient sources are reflected, for example, in *Ethics of Rhetoric*, 128, 174, 203; *Composition*, 212; and "Language Is Sermonic," 62. Chapter one of *Ethics of Rhetoric* is a perceptive analysis of Plato's *Phaedrus*.

[34] Weaver, "Concealed Rhetoric in Scientistic Sociology," 20–24, 28–30; *Ethics of Rhetoric*, 12, 22, 128, 225; "Language Is Sermonic," 60–61; *Composition*, 43; *Visions of Order*, 105; *Life Without Prejudice*, 46–47.

[35] "Concealed Rhetoric in Scientistic Sociology," 20, 22.

[36] *Life Without Prejudice*, 116–18.

involves questions of policy. It operates formally at the point "where literary values and political urgencies" can be combined. "The rhetorician," he observed, "makes use of the moving power of literary presentation to induce in his hearers an attitude or decision which is political in the very broadest sense."[37]

Weaver explained the "office" of rhetoric at some length: "Rhetoric seen in the whole conspectus of its function is an art of emphasis embodying an order of desire. Rhetoric is advisory; it has the office of advising men with reference to an independent order of goods and with reference to their particular situation as it relates to these. The honest rhetorician therefore has two things in mind: a vision of how matters should go ideally and ethically and a consideration of the special circumstances of his auditors. Toward both of these he has a responsibility."[38] The duty of rhetoric, then, is to combine "action and understanding into a whole that is greater than scientific perception." Weaver the Platonic idealist believed that "rhetoric at its truest seeks to perfect men by showing them better versions of themselves, links in that chain extending up toward the ideal which only the intellect can apprehend and only the soul have affection for."[39]

Rhetoric, held Weaver, is axiological; it kneads values into our lives.[40] Rhetoric is the cohesive force that molds

[37] *Ethics of Rhetoric*, 16, 17, 115; "Language Is Sermonic," 63.

[38] "Language Is Sermonic," 54. Rhetoric must integrate the realms of Ideas and Particulars, of Being and Becoming.

[39] *Ethics of Rhetoric*, 24–25. The infusion of Weaver's philosophy into his view of rhetoric bears out his premise that our "conception of metaphysical reality finally governs our conception of everything else." *Ideas Have Consequences*, 51.

[40] *Ethics of Rhetoric*, 18, 23, 24, 211; "Language Is Sermonic," 58, 60–63; *Ideas Have Consequences*, 3, 19–20, 153, 167; *Visions of Order*, 67–69, 135; *Life Without Prejudice*, 118. Weaver made a detailed analysis of ultimate "god terms" and "devil terms" which have potency in contemporary American discourse. See *Ethics of Rhetoric*, 211–32.

persons into a community or culture. Because man is "drawn forward by some conception of what he should be," a proper order of values is the "ultimate sanction of rhetoric." Rhetoric involves the making and presenting of choices among "goods" and a striving toward some ultimate Good. By its very nature, he emphasized, "language is sermonic"; it reflects choices and urges a particular "ought." The "noble rhetorician," in Weaver's view, functions to provide a better vision of what we can become. The true rhetorician attempts to actualize an "ideal good" for a particular audience in a specific situation primarily through "poetic or analogical association." He demonstrates, for instance, how an action, urged as just, partakes of ideal justice.

Weaver, therefore, condemned most social scientists for pretending to avoid value judgments in their writings while actually making such judgments.[41] He particularly attacked general semantics for its relativistic "truth" and its attempt to denude language of all reflections of value tendencies.[42] He also realized that rhetoric can be perverted to employ base techniques and to serve base ends. Such perversion, he believed, occurs in much modern advertising. Against these possibilities Weaver strove in all his writings on rhetoric. For he was certain that "all things considered, rhetoric, noble or base, is a great power in the world."[43]

Like Aristotle, Weaver perceived a close relationship be-

[41] "Concealed Rhetoric in Scientistic Sociology," 19–32. Weaver also analyzed the "sources of pervasive vices" in the rhetoric of social scientists, sources which make their prose difficult to understand and seemingly divorced from reality. See *Ethics of Rhetoric,* Chap. 8.

[42] *Ideas Have Consequences,* 4–5, 150–60; *Visions of Order,* 67–70; "Relativism and the Use of Language," 236–54; Weaver, "To Write the Truth," 25–30.

[43] *Ethics of Rhetoric,* 11–12, 18–24, 217, 232; *Ideas Have Consequences,* 153; *Life Without Prejudice,* 121–28.

tween dialectic and rhetoric.[44] Dialectic, he maintained, is a "method of investigation whose object is the establishment of truth about doubtful propositions." It is "abstract reasoning" upon the basis of propositions through categorization, definition, drawing out of implications, and exposure of contradictions. Dialectic involves analysis and synthesis of fundamental terms in controversial questions. Both dialectic and rhetoric operate in the realm of probability. Rhetoric is joined with "that branch of dialectic which contributes to choice or avoidance"—that branch of dialectic which examines ethical and political questions. Good rhetoric presupposes sound dialectic. A successful dialectic secures not actuality but possibility; "what rhetoric thereafter accomplishes is to take any dialectically secured position . . . and show its relationship to the world of prudential conduct."[45] Weaver's criticism of the semantic positivists suggests that dialectic alone, without a succeeding rhetoric, is "social agnosticism." With dialectic unaided by rhetoric, man "knows" only in a vacuum. Thus, as earlier noted, "the duty of rhetoric is to bring together action and understanding into a whole that is greater than scientific perception." Rhetoric seeks actualization of a dialectically secured position in the existential world.

Weaver knew that logos, pathos, and ethos must combine in sound rhetoric.[46] For him "the most obvious truth about rhetoric is that its object is the whole man." It

[44] *Ethics of Rhetoric*, 15–22, 25, 27–29; *Composition*, 120–23; *Visions of Order*, 55–72. For an example of Weaver's use of dialectic see *Visions of Order*, 92–112. As a rhetorical critic, he analyzed the use of rhetoric and dialectic by John Randolph of Roanoke, Henry David Thoreau, and by Bryan and Darrow in the Scopes Trial. See *Life Without Prejudice*, 65–97; *Ethics of Rhetoric*, Chap. 2.

[45] *Ethics of Rhetoric*, 27–28.

[46] "Language Is Sermonic," 51, 59–60; *Ethics of Rhetoric*, 134; *Ideas Have Consequences*, 19, 21, 165–67; *Visions of Order*, 70–72.

presents its arguments first to the rational aspect of man. Yet a complete rhetoric goes beyond man's cognitive capacity and appeals to other facets of his nature, especially to his nature as an emotional being, "a being of feeling and suffering." In addition, he realized that a "significant part of every speech situation is the character of the speaker." For Richard Weaver, then, the function of rhetoric was to make men both feel and believe and to perceive order, first principles, and fundamental values.

He seemed committed to the proposition that as a man speaks, so he is—or that style is the man. A person's typical modes of argument and his stylistic characteristics Weaver saw as keys to that person's philosophical orientation. An analysis of a person's rhetorical style, for example, illuminated his world view.[47] Frequent use of the conjunction "but" indicates, for example, a "balanced view" as a habit of mind. Again: A person's level of generality in word choice tells us something about his approach to a subject.

"A man's method of argument is a truer index of his beliefs than his explicit profession of principles," Weaver held as a basic axiom.[48] "A much surer index to a man's political philosophy," he felt, "is his characteristic way of thinking, inevitably expressed in the type of argument he prefers." Nowhere does a man's rhetoric catch up with him more completely than in "the topics he chooses to win other men's assent." At one point Weaver elaborated his fundamental view at some length:

[47] *Ethics of Rhetoric*, 115–42, 167. As a rhetorical critic, Weaver used a stylistic analysis to probe the "heroic" prose of John Milton and to illuminate the "spaciousness" of American oratory in the 1840's and 1850's. See *Ethics of Rhetoric*, Chaps. 5 and 6.

[48] This and the following quotations are from *Ethics of Rhetoric*, 58, 112, 114, 55.

In other words, the rhetorical content of the major premise which the speaker habitually uses is the key to his primary view of existence. We are of course excluding artful choices which have in view only *ad hoc* persuasions. Putting the matter now figuratively, we may say that no man escapes being branded by the premise that he regards as most efficacious in argument. The general importance of this is that major premises, in addition to their logical function as a part of a deductive argument, are expressive of values, and a characteristic major premise characterizes the user.[49]

From the Aristotelian *topoi* Weaver selected and ranked certain "topics" or regions of experience to which an advocate could turn for the substance of persuasive argument. These "topics" are the "sources of content for speeches that are designed to influence."[50] By ranking them from the most to least ethically desirable, based on his philosophic conception of reality and knowledge, he outlined a hierarchy of topics which a persuader might use and which a critic could employ to assess the rhetoric of others.[51]

A speaker would make the highest order of appeal by basing his argument on genus or definition.[52] Argument from genus involves arguing from the nature or essence of things. It assumes that there are fixed classes and that what

---

[49] *Ibid.*, 55–56. Although Weaver excludes "artful choices," the point can be raised that rhetoric by definition is artful in its adaptation to audience and situation and in its conscious effort at success. For an interesting attempt to test Weaver's axiom, without prior knowledge of Weaver's view, see Edwin S. Shneidmann, "The Logic of Politics," in Leon Arons and Mark May (eds.), *Television and Human Behavior* (New York: Appleton-Century-Crofts, 1963), 177–99.

[50] "Language Is Sermonic," 53; *Composition*, 124.

[51] "Language Is Sermonic," 55.

[52] *Ibid.*, 53, 55–56; *Composition*, 124–27; *Ethics of Rhetoric*, 27, 56, 112–14; *Visions of Order*, 6. For Weaver's own extensive use of argument from genus or definition see, for example, *Ideas Have Consequences*, 43–44, 101, 129, 172; *Visions of Order*, Chaps. 1, 2, and 8.

is true of a given class may be imputed to every member of that class. In the argument from genus the classification already is established, or it is one of the fixed concepts in the mind of the audience to which the argument is addressed. In argument from definition, the work of establishing the classification must be done during the course of the argument, after which the defined term will be used as would a genus. Further: Definitions should be rationally rather than empirically sustained. Good definitions should be stipulative, emphasizing what-ought-to-be, rather than operational, emphasizing what-is. Under argument from genus or definition, Weaver also included argument from fundamental principles and argument from example. An example, he felt, always implies a general class. He believed that arguments from genus or definition ascribe "to the highest reality qualities of stasis, immutability, eternal perdurance."

He admitted that his preference for this mode of argument derived from his Platonic idealism. This mode of argument, he felt, was also a mark of the true conservative. To argue from genus or definition was to get people "to see what is most permanent in existence, or what transcends the world of change and accident. The realm of essence is the realm above the flux of phenomena; and definitions are of essences and genera."[53]

Weaver applied this viewpoint in his evaluation of the rhetoric of Abraham Lincoln.[54] He explicitly cited over a

[53] "Language Is Sermonic," 55; *Life Without Prejudice*, 158–59.
[54] *Ethics of Rhetoric*, 85–114. The user of arguments from genus, principle, and definition often realizes that on some issues there is no middle ground, only right and wrong. Lincoln, for instance, knew that honesty and long-run political success on the slavery issue depended upon avoiding major middle-road positions. But the failure of Stephen Douglas on the slavery question, believed Weaver, was that he chose an untenable position in the "excluded middle." See *Ethics of Rhetoric*, 94–95, 105–107.

dozen examples of Lincoln's rhetoric. Yet unfortunately he did not indicate whether he based his generalizations on a careful examination of the entire corpus of the martyred President's oratory. Weaver's analysis led him to conclude that, although sometimes arguing from similitude, as in the Gettysburg Address, and again from consequence and circumstance, Lincoln characteristically argued from genus, definition, and principle. His greatest utterances, for example, were "chiefly arguments from definition." And in Weaver's view, therefore, Lincoln was a true conservative.[55] In contrast, many of Lincoln's contemporary Whigs were conservative, Weaver argued, only in the negative sense that they opposed Democratic proposals. Naturally Weaver praised Lincoln's rhetoric and his philosophical position.

As second in rank among the topics Weaver placed argument from similitude.[56] In this mode of argument are embraced analogy, metaphor, figuration, comparison, and contrast. Metaphor received focused attention from Weaver; to him it was often central to the rhetorical process.[57] Some of our profoundest intuitions concerning the world around us, he noted, are expressed in the form of comparisons. His Platonic idealism again helped him rank this topic. The user of an analogy hints at an essence he cannot at the moment produce. Weaver asserted that "behind every analogy lurks the possibility of a general term."

Argument from cause and effect stands third in Weaver's

---

[55] Weaver saw George Washington as the "archetypal American conservative." *Life Without Prejudice*, 165.

[56] "Language Is Sermonic," 53, 56; *Ethics of Rhetoric*, 56–57; *Composition*, 129–32. For examples of Weaver's own use of argument from similitude see *Visions of Order*, Chaps. 2 and 7.

[57] *Ethics of Rhetoric*, 18, 23, 127–35, 150–52, 202–206; *Composition*, 248–58; *Visions of Order*, 142.

hierarchy of topics, and includes argument from consequences.[58] Although causal reasoning is a "less exalted"
source of argument, we "all have to use it because we are
historical men." This method of argument and its subvarieties, he felt, characterized the radical and the pragmatist.
Causal argument operates in the realm of "becoming" and
thus in the realm of flux. Argument from consequences
attempts to forecast results of some course of action, either
very desirable or very undesirable. These results are a determining factor for one in deciding whether or not to adopt a
proposed action. Arguments from consequences, Weaver
observed, usually are completely "devoid of reference to
principle or defined ideas."

At the very bottom of Weaver's hierarchy stands argument from circumstances, another subvariety of causal
reasoning.[59] This mode of argument, in his view, is the least
"philosophical" of the topics because it admits of the least
perspicaciousness and theoretically stops at the level of
perception of fact. Argument from circumstances characterizes those who are easily impressed by existing tangibles,
and such argument marks, he believed, the true liberal.[60]
The arguers from circumstance, concerned not with "con-
·ceptions of verities but qualities of perceptions," lack moral

---

[58] "Language Is Sermonic," 53, 56; *Composition*, 127–28; *Ethics of Rhetoric*, 57; *Life Without Prejudice*, 142, 145; Weaver, "A Responsible Rhetoric," (Address delivered March 29, 1955, to a Great Issues Forum of students at Purdue University), 4. See *Visions of Order*, Chaps. 1 and 2, for examples of his use of causal reasoning. And to a degree his *Ideas Have Consequences* is an argument from consequences; violation of cer-tain ideals, values, and principles has led to destructive consequences.
[59] "Language Is Sermonic," 57; *Ethics of Rhetoric*, 57–58; *Composition*, 128–29; *Ideas Have Consequences*, 151. An example of Weaver's infre-quent personal usage is in *Ideas Have Consequences*, 134.
[60] Weaver's major redefinition of the terms "liberal" and "conservative" seems to violate the type of linguistic covenant which he espouses as neces-sary in "Relativism and the Use of Language," 247–53.

vision and possess only the illusion of reality. We are driven back upon this method of argument when a course of action cannot be vindicated by principle or when effects cannot be demonstrated. The argument simply cites brute circumstance; it suggests expediency. "Actually," he explains, "this argument amounts to a surrender of reason. Maybe it expresses an instinctive feeling that in this situation reason is powerless. Either you change fast or you get crushed. But surely it would be a counsel of desperation to try only this argument in a world suffering from aimlessness and threatened with destruction."[61]

Weaver employed this topic to analyze the rhetoric of Edmund Burke, commonly classified as a conservative.[62] He conceded that many of Burke's observations on society have a conservative basis. On the other hand, he contended that when Burke came to grips with concrete policies, his rhetoric reflected "a strong addiction to the argument from circumstance." Weaver concluded, "When judged by what we are calling aspect of argument," Burke was "very far from being a conservative."[63] Burke was at his best, Weaver argued, when defending immediate circumstances and "reigning" circumstances. And until the time of the French Revolution when he felt the need for "deeper anchorage," Burke's habitual argument from circumstances marked him philosophically as a liberal.[64] Weaver held Burke in low esteem as a conservative.

Again, while Weaver cited some dozen examples of

[61] "Language Is Sermonic," 57.
[62] *Ethics of Rhetoric*, 55–84; Weaver, "The People of the Excluded Middle" (unpublished and undated manuscript), 12. Weaver felt that although circumstance was no more than a retarding factor in Lincoln's considerations, circumstance was for Burke the deciding factor. See *Ethics of Rhetoric*, 95.
[63] *Ethics of Rhetoric*, 58.
[64] "The People of the Excluded Middle," 12.

Burke's rhetoric, he failed to indicate whether his generalizations rested on a scrutiny of all Burke's speeches, letters, and essays. It is in this connection also worthy of note that Russell Kirk has levied several objections to Weaver's evaluation of Burke.[65] First, the true conservative described by Weaver, contends Kirk, represents Weaver's *ideal* and ignores the historical fact that a true conservative is a follower of Edmund Burke, no matter what his typical mode of argument. Second, Kirk alludes to one of Burke's speeches to indicate that while Burke disdained "abstraction," he did praise genuine "principle." Here Kirk ignores Weaver's axiom that the important index is not what one says, but how one characteristically argues. Third, Kirk claims that although Abraham Lincoln often may have argued from principles and definition, he also often acted from circumstances and consequences. Finally, Kirk sees Burke's prosecution of Warren Hastings and his attack on French errors during the Revolution as "instances of argument and action from definition."

Weaver's central premise of a typical pattern of argument for a speaker implies simple frequency of usage, as reflected in his use of the terms "characteristic" and "habitual." But some speakers may not have a clearly predominant mode of argument; they may blend a number of types of argument mentioned by Weaver. Judgment of the speaker is then more difficult. More important, some speakers may use arguments from consequences and circumstances more frequently than other types and yet use a few arguments from genus or principle as the fundamental arguments underlying all others.[66] Finally, Weaver fails to

---

[65] Russell Kirk, "Ethical Labor," 485–503.
[66] See, for example, Richard L. Johannesen, "John Quincy Adams' Speaking on Territorial Expansion, 1836–1848" (Ph.D. dissertation: University of Kansas, 1964), 304–50.

explain how a critic may determine whether a given line of argument is a metaphysical choice reflecting a speaker's philosophical stance or an "artful" choice necessitated by the practicalities of audience adaptation.

The use of characteristic mode of argument as the prime standard for rhetorical criticism represents an overly simplistic approach to evaluation of rhetorical practice. Such analysis promotes the slighting of other relevant factors in the rhetorical process. In the dramatistic terms proposed by Kenneth Burke, Weaver overemphasizes "agency" at the expense of "agent," "act," "scene," and "purpose." His typology of the "aspect" of argument can afford valuable insights, but it must not be taken as a well-rounded critical system. Yet in fairness to him it must be admitted that he did not intend his system to serve as the universal criterion for rhetorical criticism.

In addition to the hierarchy of "internal" sources of argument is the "external topic" of argument from authority and testimony.[67] Statements made by observers and experts take the place of direct or logical interpretation of evidence. Such testimony often embodies arguments from genus or definition, cause-effect, consequences, and circumstances, and thus can be judged by the standards appropriate to such arguments. But also involved is the more general question of the status of the authority. Thus a sound criterion, wrote Weaver, is that an argument from authority is only as good as the authority itself.

In his writing and teaching Weaver constantly strove to train his students in ethical rhetoric. Hence knowledge of rhetoric and skill in its use provided a defense against base rhetoric and propaganda.[68] In rhetorical education he

---

[67] "Language Is Sermonic," 54, 57; *Composition*, 132–34.
[68] *Composition*, iii–iv; *Ethics of Rhetoric*, 232; "To Write the Truth," 25–30.

placed prime emphasis on invention and style. Argumentation, including induction, deduction, and a modernized set
of *topoi* adapted from Aristotle, formed a crucial part of
rhetorical education.[69] The enthymeme received focused
attention in Weaver's philosophy of rhetoric.[70] The rhetorician, he observed, enters into a oneness with his audience
by tacitly agreeing with one of its perceptions of reality.
Weaver noted further that the enthymeme functions only
when the "audience is willing to supply the missing proposition."[71]

In *Composition*, a college textbook, Weaver treated the
following "topics": genus or definition, cause and effect,
similitude, comparison, contraries, circumstance, testimony, and authority. As could be expected, a major part of
Weaver's text was devoted to style, including grammar and
composition. His persistent efforts stimulated introduction
of units on logic and the revitalized "topics" into the
freshman English course in the College of the University of
Chicago.[72]

Edward P. J. Corbett credits the article by Bilsky,
Weaver, and others in *College English* (in 1953)—"Looking for an Argument"—with providing "perhaps the first

[69] *Composition*, 90–120, 123–34.
[70] *Ethics of Rhetoric*, 173–74; *Visions of Order*, 63–64; *Composition*,
118–20; "Concealed Rhetoric in Scientist Sociology," 29–31.
[71] For a similar view see Lloyd Bitzer, "Aristotle's Enthymeme Revisited,"
Quarterly Journal of Speech, XLV (December, 1959), 399–408. American
oratory in the 1840's and 1850's was characterized by the use of "uncontested terms" and ideas "fixed by universal consensus" as unstated
premises already accepted by audiences. This characteristic marked the
"spaciousness" of the rhetoric of that era. See *Ethics of Rhetoric*, 164–74.
[72] Ebbitt, "Richard M. Weaver, Teacher of Rhetoric," 417. Insight into
argumentation and the *topoi* as taught to the freshman is gained from
Manuel Bilsky, McCrea Hazlett, Robert Streeter, and Richard Weaver,
"Looking for an Argument," *College English*, XIV (January, 1953), 210–
16. Many of Weaver's personal classroom concerns are reflected in an
unpublished paper, "The Place of Logic in the English Curriculum."

suggestion of the value of classical rhetoric for the Freshman Composition course." Corbett claims that the treatment of the *topoi* in Weaver's *Composition* "represented the first instance of the use of the topics in a freshman rhetoric since the appearance of Francis P. Donnelly's books in the 1930's."[73]

Weaver's writings on rhetoric emphasize the processes and techniques of invention and the elements of effective style, giving minor place to organization and none to the classical canons of delivery and memory. He aims indeed at revitalizing invention and argumentation. To Weaver true rhetoric involves choices among values and courses of action; it aims at showing men "better versions of themselves" and better visions of an ultimate Good. As Platonic idealist and political conservative, he praised the ideal, the essence, the unchangeable, and condemned the particular, the transitory, and the expedient. A speaker's characteristic use of argument from genus, definition, principle, similitude, cause and effect, consequences, and circumstances, Weaver regarded as an index to the speaker's philosophical viewpoint and ethical stature.

By reaffirming and refining the essential connection between dialectic and rhetoric, Weaver illuminated the true province of rhetoric. Indeed, Weaver's theory pointed the way to the current rapprochement between philosophy and rhetoric.[74] Some of Weaver's political, philosophical, and rhetorical assumptions may be questioned in whole or in

[73] Edward P. J. Corbett, "Rhetoric and Teachers of English," *Quarterly Journal of Speech*, LI (December, 1965), 380.

[74] Natanson, "The Limits of Rhetoric," 136–37. Witness the increased recent interest in scholarly scrutiny of philosophical-rhetorical issues. See, for example, Otis Walter, "On Views of Rhetoric, Whether Conservative or Progressive," *Quarterly Journal of Speech*, XLIX (December, 1963), 367–82, and the journal, *Philosophy and Rhetoric*, published by the Pennsylvania State University Press.

part. Still, there is little doubt that Weaver's theory, rooted as it was in a dialectic of the "true nature of things," has helped to reestablish rhetoric as a substantive discipline —a discipline concerned with matters of "the real world" and with the preservation of "the permanent things."

Richard M. Weaver
on the Nature of Rhetoric

The rhetorician hopes that words will move man. . . . Rhetoric takes into account history and circumstances, things felt by the heart, while dialectic remains neutral.

> —RICHARD M. WEAVER, unpublished lecture
> delivered at the University of Arkansas
> *November 8, 1961*

Richard Weaver wrote "The Power of the Word" in defense of language as the vehicle of order—as the touchstone to enduring human values and universal truths. The theme is a recurring one, central to Weaver's conception of the role of rhetoric. This statement is, in final analysis, a rebuttal to S. I. Hayakawa and the general semanticists' abandonment of "ontological referents" and their attempt to "substitute things for words." Weaver felt strongly that modern man's confusion and sense of moral helplessness grew from his "failure to insist upon no compromise in definition." Here is Weaver's affirmation of the "philosophical quality of language" and of "the power of the word to define and compel."

The corruption of man is followed by the corruption of language.

—EMERSON

The Power
of the Word

AFTER SECURING a place in the world from which to fight, we should turn our attention first to the matter of language. The impulse to dissolve everything into sensation has made powerful assaults against the forms which enable discourse, because these institute a discipline and operate through predications which are themselves fixities. We have sought an ultimate sanction for man's substance in metaphysics, and we must do the same for his language if we are to save it from a similar prostitution. All metaphysical community depends on the ability of men to understand one another.

At the beginning I should urge examining in all seriousness that ancient belief that a divine element is present in language. The feeling that to have power of language is to have control over things is deeply imbedded in the human mind. We see this in the way men gifted in speech are feared or admired; we see it in the potency ascribed to incantations, interdictions, and curses. We see it in the legal force given to oath or word. A man can bind himself in the face of contingencies by saying Yea or Nay, which can only mean that words in common human practice express something transcending the moment. Speech is, moreover, the vehicle of order, and those who command it are regarded as having superior insight, which must be into the necessary relationship of things. Such is the philosophic meaning of great myths. "And out of the ground the Lord God formed every beast of the field, and every fowl of the air; and brought them unto Adam to see what he would call them, and whatever Adam called every living creature, that was the name thereof." This story symbolizes the fact that man's overlordship begins with the naming of the world. Having named the animals, he has in a sense ordered them, and what other than a classified catalogue of names is a large part of natural science? To discover what a thing is "called" according to some system is the essential step in knowing, and to say that all education is learning to name rightly, as Adam named the animals, would assert an underlying truth. The sentence passed upon Babel confounded the learning of its builders.

As myth gives way to philosophy in the normal sequence we have noted, the tendency to see a principle of divinity in language endures. Thus we learn that in the late ancient world the Hebrew *memra* and the Greek *logos* merged, and in the Gospel of John we find an explicit identification:

> In the beginning was the Word, and
> the Word was with God, and the Word was God.
> The same was in the beginning with God.

A following verse declares that *logos* as god lies behind the design of the cosmos, for "without him was not anything made that was made." Speech begins to appear the principle of intelligibility. So when wisdom came to man in Christ, in continuation of this story, "the Word was made flesh and dwelt among us." The allegory need give no difficulty; knowledge of the prime reality comes to man through the word; the word is a sort of deliverance from the shifting world of appearances. The central teaching of the New Testament is that those who accept the word acquire wisdom and at the same time some identification with the eternal, usually figured as everlasting life.

It seems that man, except in periods of loss of confidence, when skepticism impugns the very possibility of knowledge, shows thus an incurable disposition to look upon the word as a means of insight into the noumenal world. The fact that language is suprapersonal, uniting countless minds which somehow stand in relationship to an overruling divinity, lies at the root of this concept. If, as Karl Vossler has observed, "Everything that is spoken on this globe in the course of ages must be thought of as a vast soliloquy spoken by the human mind, which unfolds itself in millions of persons and characters, and comes to itself again in their reunion," language must somehow express the enduring part. Certainly one of the most important revelations about a period comes in its theory of language, for that informs us whether language is viewed as a bridge to the noumenal or as a body of fictions convenient for grappling with transitory phenomena. Not without point is the cynical observation of Hobbes that "words are wise men's counters—they do but reckon by them—but they are the money of fools." Doctrines thus sharply defined can tell us whether a period is idealistic or pragmatic. Because this circumstance concerns the problem of restoration at a critical point, it becomes necessary to say something about contemporary theories of language.

The most notable development of our time in the province of language study is the heightened interest in semantics, which seems to stem from a realization that words, after all, have done things on their own, so to express it. I shall review briefly the state of the question. The problem of the word was argued with great acuteness by the Middle Ages, and one of the first major steps in the direction of modern skepticism came through the victory of Occam over Aquinas in a controversy about language. The statement that *modi essendi et subsistendi* were replaced by *modi significandi et intelligendi,* or that ontological referents were abandoned in favor of pragmatic significations, describes broadly the change in philosophy which continues to our time. From Occam to Bacon, from Bacon to Hobbes, and from Hobbes to contemporary semanticists, the progression is clear: ideas become psychological figments, and words become useful signs.

Semantics, which I shall treat as an extreme outgrowth of nominalism, seems inspired by two things: a feeling that language does not take into account the infinite particularity of the world and a phobia in the face of the autonomous power of words.

The semanticists are impressed with the world as process, and, feeling with Heraclitus that no man can step in the same river twice, they question how the fixities of language can represent a changeful reality. S. I. Hayakawa, one of the best-known popularizers of the subject, tells us that "the universe is in a perpetual state of flux."[1] Alfred Korzybski has declared that the use of the word "is," in the sense condemned in his system of semantics, so falsifies the world that it could endanger our sanity. Such men work laboriously to show by categories of referents all the things

---

[1] *Language in Action,* 121.

a single term can mean, and, at the same time, they take into account the circumstances of the user, apparently in an effort to correlate him with the world of becoming. (This should recall the earlier tendency of Romanticism to regard a work of art as expressive of the artist's emotional condition at the moment of its execution.) They desire language to reflect not conceptions of verities but qualities of perceptions, so that man may, by the pragmatic theory of success, live more successfully. To one completely committed to this realm of becoming, as are the empiricists, the claim to apprehend verities is a sign of psychopathology. Probably we have here but a highly sophisticated expression of the doctrine that ideals are hallucinations and that the only normal, sane person is the healthy extrovert, making instant, instinctive adjustments to the stimuli of the material world. To such people as these, Christ as preacher of the Word, is a "homosexual paranoiac." In effect, their doctrine seems part of the general impulse to remove all barriers to immediate apprehension of the sensory world, and so one must again call attention to a willingess to make the physical the sole determinant of what is.

In recognizing that words have power to define and to compel, the semanticists are actually testifying to the philosophic quality of language which is the source of their vexation. In an attempt to get rid of that quality, they are looking for some neutral means which will be a nonconductor of the current called "emotion" and its concomitant of evaluation. They are introducing into language, in the course of their prescriptions, exactly the same atomization which we have deplored in other fields. They are trying to strip words of all meaning that shows tendency, or they are trying to isolate language from the noumenal world by ridding speech of tropes.

Let us consider an illustration from Hayakawa's *Language in Action*, a work which has done much to put the new science before the public. It is easy to visualize a social situation, the author tells us, in which payment to unemployed persons will be termed by one group of citizens "relief" and by another "social insurance." One can admit the possibility, but what lies behind the difference in terminology? The answer is: a conception of ends which evaluates the tendency of the action named. The same sort of thing is encountered when one has to decide whether the struggle of the American colonists against Great Britain should be termed a "rebellion" or a "war for independence." In the first case, the bare existential thing, the payment of money to needy persons (and it will be noted that this translation does not purify the expression of tendency) is like anything else neutral as long as we consider it solely with reference to material and efficient causes. But, when we begin to think about what it represents in the totality, it takes on new attributes (emotional loading, these may be called) causing people to divide according to their sentiments or their metaphysical dream.

It is in such instances that the semanticists seem to react hysterically to the fear of words. Realizing that today human beings are in disagreement as never before and that words serve to polarize the conflicting positions, they propose an ending of polarity. I have mentioned, earlier, people who are so frightened over the existence of prejudice that they are at war with simple predication. The semanticists see in every epithet a prejudice.

The point at issue is explained by a fundamental proposition of Aquinas: "Every form is accompanied by an inclination." Now language is a system of forms, which both singly and collectively have this inclination or intention.

The aim of semantics is to dissolve form and thereby destroy inclination in the belief that the result will enable a scientific manipulation. Our argument is that the removal of inclination destroys the essence of language.

Let us look more closely at the consequence of taking all tendentious meaning from speech. It is usually supposed that we would then have a scientific, objective vocabulary, which would square with the "real" world and so keep us from walking into stone walls or from fighting one another over things that have no existence. Actually the result would be to remove all teleology, for language would no longer have *nisus*, and payment to the needy would be neither "relief" nor "social insurance" but something without character, which we would not know how to place in our scheme of values. (The fact that equalitarian democracy, to the extent that it makes leadership superfluous or impossible, is repudiating teleology must not be overlooked here. Teleology enjoins from above; equalitarian democracy takes its counsel without point of reference. The advantage of semantics to equalitarian democracy is pointed out by some semanticists.)

Hayakawa has said further that "arguments over intensional meaning can result only in irreconcilable conflict."[2] With the proper qualifications, this observation is true. Since language expresses tendency, and tendency has direction, those who differ over tendency can remain at harmony only in two ways: (1) by developing a complacency which makes possible the ignoring of contradictions and (2) by referring to first principles, which will finally remove the difference at the expense of one side. If truth exists and is attainable by man, it is not to be expected that

---

[2] *Ibid.*, 63.

there will be unison among those who have different degrees of it. This is one of the painful conditions of existence which the bourgeoisie like to shut from their sight. I see no reason to doubt that here is the meaning of the verses in Scripture: "Suppose ye that I am come to give peace on earth? I tell you, Nay; but rather division" and "I bring not peace, but a sword." It was the mission of the prophet to bring a metaphysical sword among men which has been dividing them ever since, with a division that affirms value. But amid this division there can be charity, and charity is more to be relied on to prevent violence than are the political neofanaticisms of which our age is signally productive. Positivism cannot grant theology's basis of distinction, but neither can it provide a ground for charity.

When we look more narrowly at the epistemological problem raised by the semanticists, we conclude that they wish to accept patterns only from external reality. With many of them the notion seems implicit that language is an illusion or a barrier between us and what we must cope with. "Somewhere bedrock beneath words must be reached," is a common theme. Some talk about achieving an infinite-valued orientation (this last would of course leave both certitude and the idea of the good impossible). Mr. Thurman Arnold, who seems to have assimilated most of the superficial doctrines of the day, takes a stand in the *Folklore of Capitalism* even against definition. He argues that every writer on social institutions "should try to choose words and illustrations which will arouse the proper mental associations with his readers. If he doesn't succeed with them, he should try others. If he is ever led into an attempt at definition, he is lost." On the same footing of ingenuousness is another observation in this work: "When men begin to examine philosophies and principles as they examine atoms and electrons, the road to the discovery of the means of social control is open." The author of *Political Semantics*, fearful of the intervention of abstractions, suggests that the reader, too, add something to the definition given, a notion savoring strongly of progressive education. "Possibly the reader himself should participate in the process of building up a definition. Instead of being presented with finished summary definitions he might first be introduced to an array of examples arranged in such a way as to suggest the 'mental picture' in terms of which the examples were chosen."[3] There is just enough here to suggest the Socratic method; but the true implication is that there are no real definitions; there are only the general pictures one arrives at after more or less induction. The entire process is but a climbing-down of the ladder of abstraction.

Now whether it is profitable to descend that ladder is certainly not a question to be begged. Semanticists imagine, apparently, that the descent is a way out of that falsity which universality imposes on all language. Do we know more definitely what a horse is when we are in a position to point to one than when we merely use the name "horse" in its generic significance? This concerns one of the most fundamental problems of philosophy—one on which we must take a stand; and I am ready to assert that we can never break out of the circle of language and seize the object barehanded, as it were, or without some ideational operation.

It must surely be granted that whatever is unique defies definition. Definition then must depend on some kind of analogical relationship of a thing with other things, and

---

[3] Norman H. Hinton, *Political Semantics*, 68.

this can mean only that definition is ultimately circular. That is to say, if one begins defining a word with synonyms, he will, if he continues, eventually complete a circuit and arrive at the very terms with which he started. Suppose we allow Korzybski, who has been especially restive in what appears to him the imprisoning net of language, to testify from his experiments: "We begin by asking the 'meaning' of every word uttered, being satisfied for this purpose with the roughest definition; then we ask the 'meaning' of the words used in the definition, and this process is continued for no more than ten to fifteen minutes, until the victim begins to speak in circles as, for instance, defining 'space' by 'length' and 'length' by 'space.' When this stage is reached, we have usually come to the *undefined* terms of the given individual. If we still press, no matter how gently, for definitions, a most interesting fact occurs. Sooner or later, signs of affective disturbance appear. Often the face reddens; there is body restlessness—symptoms quite similar to those seen in a schoolboy who has forgotten his lessons, which he 'knows' but cannot tell. . . . Here we have reached the bottom and the foundation of all *non-elementalistic* meanings, the meanings of *undefined* terms, which we 'know' somehow but cannot tell."

Taking the experiment as Korzybski recounts it, I would wish to ask whether his schoolboy who has forgotten his lessons is not every man, whose knowledge comes by a process of recalling and who is embarrassed as by ignorance when he can no longer recall? He is here frustrated because he cannot find any further analogues to illustrate what he knows. Any person, it seems, can be driven back to that knowledge which comes to him by immediate apprehension, but the very fact of his possessing such knowledge makes him a participant in the communal mind. I do not desire to press the issue here, but I suspect that this is evidence supporting the doctrine of knowledge by recollection taught by Plato and the philosophers of the East. If we can never succeed in getting out of the circle of definition, is it not true that all conventional definitions are but reminders of what we already, in a way, possess? The thing we have never heard of is defined for us by the things we know; putting these together, we discover, or unbury, the concept which was there all the while. If, for example, a class in science is being informed that "ontogeny recapitulates phylogeny," it is only being asked to synthesize concepts already more or less familiar. Finding the meaning of the *definiendum* is finding what emerges naturally if our present concepts are put together in the right relation. Even empirical investigations of the learning process bear this out. Such conclusions lead to the threshold of a significant commitment: ultimate definition is, as Aristotle affirmed, a matter of intuition. Primordial conception is somehow in us; from this we proceed as already noted by analogy, or the process of finding resemblance to one thing in another.[4]

[4] It may be objected at this point that I have chosen to deal with the popularizers of semantics, with men who have cheapened or distorted the science. Because this work is a study in social consequences, it is necessary to look at the form in which these doctrines reach the public. There is, of course, a group of serious philosophers who are working at language with caution and a sense of responsibility and who believe that they are erecting for us important safeguards against error. But, when I look into the writings of these men, I find, alas, that their conclusions march in the same direction as those of the popularizers. The Darwinian link is acknowledged, and semantics resembles, as much as before, behaviorism imported into language. Thus, Charles W. Morris in *Foundations of the Theory of Signs* stresses the importance of semantics because "it has directed attention more closely to the relation of signs to their users than had previously been done and has assessed more profoundly than ever before the relevance of this relation in understanding intellectual activities." Language is spoken of as if it were some curious development of sense which enables an organism to take into account objects not perceptually present. The determination of the scientist to see all reality as process appears later in

All this has bearing on our issue with semantics because words, each containing its universal, are our reminders of knowledge. For this reason it seems to me that semanticists are exactly wrong in regarding language as an obstruction or a series of pitfalls. Language, on the contrary, appears as a great storehouse of universal memory, or it may be said to serve as a net, not imprisoning us but supporting us and aiding us to get at a meaning beyond present meaning through the very fact that it embodies others' experiences. Words, because of their common currency, acquire a significance greater than can be imparted to them by a single user and greater than can be applied to a single situation. In this way the word is evocative of ideal aspects, which by our premises are the only aspects constituting knowledge. On this point I shall call as my witnesses two men as far apart as Shelley and a contemporary psychologist. The poet writes in *Prometheus Unbound:*

> Language is a perpetual Orphic song,
> Which rules with Daedal harmony the throng
> Of thoughts and forms, which else senseless and
>   shapeless were.

Wilbur Marshall Urban declares in *Language and Reality:* "It is part of my general thesis that all meaning is ultimately linguistic and that although science, in the interests of purer notation and manipulation, may break through the husk of language, its nonlinguistic symbols must again

---

the same work when Morris collapses the notion of "meaning" by making it purely a function of relationships. That is to say, nothing is, intrinsically, but each thing is, in terms of the process as a whole. The significant implication follows that concepts are not entities but are, rather, highly selective processes "in which the organism gets indications as to how to act with reference to the world in order to satisfy its needs or interests."

be translated back into natural language if intelligibility is to be possible."[5]

The community of language gives one access to significances at which he cannot otherwise arrive. To find a word is to find a meaning; to create a word is to find a single term for a meaning partially distributed in other words. Whoever may doubt that language has this power to evoke should try the experiment of thinking without words.

It has been necessary to make these observations because our subject is the restoration of language, and semantics has appeared to some a promising departure toward scientific reconstruction. In its seeking of objective determination, however, it turns out to represent a further flight from center. It endeavors to find the truth about reality in an agglomeration of peripheral meanings, as can be seen when its proponents insist on lowering the level of abstraction. This is only an attempt to substitute things for words, and, if words stand, in fact, for ideas, here is but the broadest aspect of our entire social disintegration. Here would be a vivid example of things in the saddle riding mankind. For the sake of memory, for the sake of logic—above all, for the sake of the unsentimental sentiment without which communities do not endure—this is a trend to be reversed. Those who regard the synthesizing power of language with horror are the atomists.

The opposition here indicated brings us necessarily to the important topic of symbolism. The attack upon the symbolic operations of language by positivists is only part of the general attack upon symbolism under way ever since it was widely agreed that there is but one world and that it is the world which is apparent to the senses. The logic is

[5] *Language and Reality*, 241. By permission of the Macmillan Company, publishers.

unexceptionable; since the symbol is a bridge to the other, the "ideational" world, those who wish to confine themselves to experience must oppose symbolism. In fact, the whole tendency of empiricism and democracy in speech, dress, and manners has been toward a plainness which is without symbolic significance. The power of symbolism is greatly feared by those who wish to expel from life all that is nonrational in the sense of being nonutilitarian, as witness the attack of Jacobins upon crowns, cassocks, and flags. As semanticists wish to plane the tropes off language, so do reformers of this persuasion wish to remove the superfluous from dress. It is worth recalling how the French Revolution simplified the dress of the Western world. At the time of this writing there appeared a report that during a leftist revolution in Bolivia the necktie was discarded as "a symbol of servility and conformity." The most tenacious in clinging to symbolic apparel have been the clerical and military callings, which we have already characterized as metaphysical; and now even the military service is under pressure to abandon its symbolic distinction in dress.

The same tendency is manifesting itself in the decay of honorifics. To the modern mind there is something so artificial and so offensive in titles of any kind that even "doctor" and "professor" are being dropped, though the military services cling grimly to their titles of rank. (There is a further lesson to be drawn from the fact that practitioners of the applied science of medicine have been allowed to keep theirs.) Honorifics are often mere flummery, to be sure, but one must not overlook the truth that they represent an effort to distinguish between men and men of parts. When not abused, they are an explicit recognition of distinction and hierarchy, a recognition that cannot be dispensed with where highly organized effort is required.

The impulse to disorganize succeeds where it makes dress and language stand for just what is before us and not for transcendental attributes or past attainments—makes us see people in an instant of time, as does the camera.[6]

The well-known fondness of the Japanese for honorific expression is but an aspect of the highly symbolic character of their culture. Natually this symbolism becomes a target for those who imagine they should re-educate the Japanese. Nothing would give the West a more complete sense of victory over the East than the abolishment of its taboos and ritualistic behavior. In this light I think we are to understand a curious press dispatch of March, 1946, which declared that MacArthur's headquarters "had suggested to the Japanese motion picture industry that kissing scenes in the movies would be a step toward democratization." We may expect many other attacks, inspired by good will and ignorance, upon the symbolic world picture of the Japanese, especially with reference to their religion and their emperor.

We return now to consider what is indicated by command over the symbolistic power of language. It is, as even primitives know, a wonderful thing to have the gift of speech. For it is true historically that those who have shown the greatest subtlety with language have shown the greatest power to understand (this does not exclude Sophists, for Plato made the point that one must be able to see the truth accurately in order to judge one's distance from it if he is practicing deception). To take a contemporary example which has statistical support: American universi-

[6] I feel certain that the Reverend John Robinson had a similar thought in mind when he enjoined the Plymouth Pilgrims to look upon their civil leaders "not beholding in them the ordinarinesse of their persons, but God's ordinance for your own good."

ties have found that with few exceptions students who display the greatest mastery of words, as evidenced by vocabulary tests and exercises in writing, make the best scholastic records regardless of the department of study they enter. For physics, for chemistry, for engineering—it matters not how superficially unrelated to language the branch of study may be—command of language will prognosticate aptitude. Facility with words bespeaks a capacity to learn relations and grasp concepts; it is a means of access to the complex reality.

Evidently it is the poet's unique command of language which gives him his ability to see the potencies in circumstances. He is the greatest teacher of cause and effect in human affairs; when Shelley declared that poets are the unacknowledged legislators of mankind, he merely signified that poets are the quickest to apprehend necessary truth. One cannot help thinking here of the peculiar fulness with which Yeats and Eliot—and, before them, Charles Péguy —foretold the present generation's leap into the abysm, and this while the falsehoods of optimism were being dinned into all ears. A poem of Eliot, "difficult" or "meaningless" in 1927, becomes today almost pat in its applications. The discourse of poetry is winged; the nominal legislators plod along empirically on foot. What can this mean except that the poet communes with the mind of the superperson? At the other extreme, those who confine their attention to the analysis of matter prove singularly inept when called upon to deal with social and political situations. If we should compile a list of those who have taught us most of what we ultimately need to know, I imagine that the scientists, for all the fanfare given them today, would occupy a rather humble place and that the dramatic poets would stand near the top.

It is difficult, therefore, to overrate the importance of skill in language. But for us there is the prior problem of preserving language itself; for, as the psyche deteriorates, language shows symptoms of malady, and today relativism, with its disbelief in truth, has made the inroads we have just surveyed upon communication. We live in an age that is frightened by the very idea of certitude, and one of its really disturbing outgrowths is the easy divorce between words and the conceptual realities which our right minds know they must stand for. This takes the form especially of looseness and exaggeration. Now exaggeration, it should be realized, is essentially a form of ignorance, one that allows and seems to justify distortion. And the psychopathic mind of war has greatly increased our addiction to this vice; indeed, during the struggle distortion became virtually the technique of reporting. A course of action, when taken by our side, was "courageous"; when taken by the enemy, "desperate"; a policy instituted by our command was "stern," or in a delectable euphemism which became popular, "rugged"; the same thing instituted by the enemy was "brutal." Seizure by military might when committed by the enemy was "conquest"; but, if committed by our side, it was "occupation" or even "liberation," so transposed did the poles become. Unity of spirit among our people was a sign of virtue; among the enemy it was a proof of incorrigible devotion to crime. The list could be prolonged indefinitely. And such always happens when men surrender to irrationality. It fell upon the Hellenic cities during the Peloponnesian War. Thucydides tells us in a vivid sentence that "the ordinary acceptation of words in their relation to things was changed as men thought fit."

Our situation would be sufficiently deplorable if such deterioration were confined to times of military conflict;

but evidence piles up that fundamental intellectual integrity, once compromised, is slow and difficult of restoration. If one examines the strikingly different significations given to "democracy" and "freedom," he is forced to realize how far we are from that basis of understanding which is prerequisite to the healing of the world. To one group "democracy" means access to the franchise; to another it means economic equality administered by a dictatorship. Or consider the number of contradictory things which have been denominated Fascist. What has happened to the one world of meaning? It has been lost for want of definers. Teachers of the present order have not enough courage to be definers; lawmakers have not enough insight.

The truth is, as we have already seen, that our surrender to irrationality has been in progress for a long time, and we witness today a breakdown of communication not only between nations and groups within nations but also between successive generations. Sir Richard Livingstone has pointed out that the people of the Western world "do not know the meaning of certain words, which had been assumed to belong to the permanent vocabulary of mankind, certain ideals which, if ignored in practice under pressure, were accepted in theory. The least important of these words is Freedom. The most important are Justice, Mercy, and Truth. In the past we have slurred this revolution over as a difference in 'ideology.' In fact it is the greatest transformation that the world has undergone, since, in Palestine or Greece, these ideals came into being or at least were recognized as principles of conduct."[7] Drift and circumstance have been permitted to change language so that the father has difficulty in speaking to the son; he endeavors to

[7] *The Future in Education* (Cambridge University Press, England), 109–10. By permission of the Macmillan Company, publishers.

speak, but he cannot make the realness of his experience evident to the child. This circumstance, as much as any other, lies behind the defeat of tradition. Progress makes father and child live in different worlds, and speech fails to provide a means to bridge them. The word is almost in limbo, where the positivists have wished to consign it.

Finally, we come to our practical undertaking. If empirical community avails nothing without the metaphysical community of language, the next step obviously is a rehabilitation of the word. That is a task for education, and the remainder of this chapter will discuss a program by which we can, I venture to hope, restore power and stability to language.

Since man necessarily uses both the poetical and the logical resources of speech, he needs a twofold training. The first part must be devoted to literature and rhetoric, the second to logic and dialectic.

The order parallels our projected scheme of things. We have shown that sentiment is the ultimate bond of community, and this we wish to secure first of all. The young come to us creatures of imagination and strong affection; they want to feel, but they do not know how—that is to say, they do not know the right objects and the right measures. And it is entirely certain that if we leave them to the sort of education obtainable today from extra-scholastic sources, the great majority will be schooled in the two vices of sentimentality and brutality. Now great poetry, rightly interpreted, is the surest antidote to both of these. In contrast with journalists and others, the great poets relate the events of history to a pure or noble metaphysical dream, which our students will have all their lives as a protecting arch over their system of values. Of course, a great deal will depend on the character and quality of the instruction. At this point I would say emphatically that we do not propose to make students chant in unison, "Life is real, life is earnest, and the grave is not its goal," though it would not be unfortunate if many emerged with that feeling. There is a sentimental poetry, and it will have to be exposed (not censored, certainly; for to omit criticism of it would deprive us of our fairest chance to combat the sentimental rhetoric of the student's environment). There may be poetry vicious in nature, and that, too, will have to be taught for what it is. But opportunity to show the affective power of words and the profound illumination which may occur through metaphor is limitless.

Let us suppose that we have set our students to studying carefully a great unsentimental poem such as Andrew Marvell's *Ode on the Return of Cromwell from Ireland*. This poem begins in a mood of innocent lyricism and passes finally to a subtle debate over the rival doctrines of revolution and legitimism. The student can be brought to see its great compression of language, achieving intense effects without exaggeration; then, perhaps, the evocation of the character of Cromwell; and, last, an enduring problem of man set in a historical context. All this is said with no implication that the poem has a "message" in the banal sense. But, if we agree that poetry is a form of knowledge, we must conclude that it does teach something, and the foregoing is a catalogue of what a student could conceivably get from one poem. Or consider the richness of Shakespeare's plays and sonnets when they are intensively read or the strange byways of sentiment—not all of them admirable, I will grant—into which the modern poets may lead a sojourner.

In brief, the discipline of poetry may be expected first to teach the evocative power of words, to introduce the student, if we may so put it, to the mighty power of symbolism, and then to show him that there are ways of feeling about things which are not provincial either in space or time. Poetry offers the fairest hope of restoring our lost unity of mind.

This part of his study should include, too, the foreign languages, and, if we really intend business, this will mean Latin and Greek. I will not list here the well-known advantages flowing from such study, but I shall mention a single one which I think has been too little regarded. Nothing so successfully discourages slovenliness in the use of language as the practice of translation. Focusing upon what a word means and then finding its just equivalent in another language compels one to look and to think before he commits himself to any expression. It is a discipline of exactness which used to be reflected in oratory and even in journalism but which is now growing as rare as considerate manners. Drill in exact translation is an excellent way of disposing the mind against that looseness and exaggeration with which the sensationalists have corrupted our world. If schools of journalism knew their business, they would graduate no one who could not render the Greek poets.

In closing, let it be added that there is a close correlation between the growth of materialism and the expulsion of languages from curricula, which is a further demonstration that where things are exalted, words will be depressed.

Our next move toward rehabilitation is the study of Socratic dialectic. I do not place dialectic second on the assumption that it provides access to regions of higher truth; it seems more likely that the symbolism of poetry does this. But, since it is impossible for men to live without reason, we must regard this as their means of coping with the datum of the world after they have established their primary feeling toward it. The laws of reason, as Spinoza said, "do but pursue the true interest and preservation of mankind." We may therefore look upon training in dialectic as our practical regimen.

The most important fact about dialectic is that it involves the science of naming. The good dialectician has come to see the world as one of choices, and he has learned to avoid that trap fatal to so many in our day, the excluded middle. It is not for him a world of undenominated things which can be combined pragmatically into any pattern. From this failure to insist upon no compromise in definition and elimination come most of our confusions. Our feeling of not understanding the world and our sense of moral helplessness are to be laid directly to an extremely subversive campaign to weaken faith in all predication. Necessity for the logical correctness of names ceases to be recognized. Until the world perceives that "good" cannot be applied to a thing because it is our own, and "bad" to the same thing because it is another's, there is no prospect of realizing community. Dialectic comes to our aid as a method by which, after our assumptions have been made, we can put our house in order. I am certain that this is why Plato in the *Cratylus* calls the giver of names a lawgiver ($\nu o \mu o \theta \epsilon \tau \eta s$); for a name, to employ his conception, is "an instrument of teaching and of distinguishing natures." But if we are to avoid confusion, the name-maker who is lawgiver cannot proceed without dialectic: "And the work of the legislator is to give names, and the dialectician must be his director if the names are to be rightly given." Plato sees here that name-giving and lawgiving are related means of effecting order. Actually stable laws require a stable vocabulary, for a principal part of every judicial process is definition, or decision about the correct name of an action. Thus the magistrates of a state have a duty to see that names are not irresponsibly changed.

In dialectic the student will get a training in definition which will compel him to see limitation and contradiction, the two things about which the philosophy of progress leaves him most confused. In effect, he will get training in thinking, whereas the best that he gets now is a vague admonition to think for himself.

Here, then, is a call for a fresh appreciation of language —perhaps, indeed, a respect for words as things. Here is an opening for education to do something more than make its customary appeal for "spiritual revival," which is itself an encouragement to diffuseness and aimlessness. If the world is to remain cosmos, we shall have to make some practical application of the law that in the beginning was the word.

Rhetoric is compulsive speech having to do with the human condition. A rhetoric without some vision of the order of the goods is actually a contradiction in terms; it would have nowhere to go, nothing to do. We cannot be too energetic in reminding our nihilists and positivists that this is a world of action and history, and that all policies involve choosing between better and worse.

—RICHARD M. WEAVER TO RALPH T. EUBANKS
January 19, 1961

Understanding the rhetoric and philosophy of Richard M. Weaver demands mastery of the ideas of "The *Phaedrus* and the Nature of Rhetoric." This, above all other works, *is* Richard M. Weaver on rhetoric. Most of what follows in his other essays flows from this interpretation of Plato's view of the right role of rhetoric. Here is the seminal statement on such important ideas as the relationship of rhetoric and dialectic, the relationship of rhetoric and axiology, the "true" and "noble" versus the "base" rhetorician, the stages of rhetorical amplification, and "semantically purified" speech. In no other of his essays is Weaver's indebtedness to the classical conception of rhetoric so apparent.

The Phaedrus *and the Nature of Rhetoric*

Our subject begins with the threshold difficulty of defining the question which Plato's *Phaedrus* was meant to answer. Students of this justly celebrated dialogue have felt uncertain of its unity of theme, and the tendency has been to designate it broadly as a discussion of the ethical and the beautiful. The explicit topics of the dialogue are, in order: love, the soul, speechmaking, and the spoken and written word, or what is generally termed by us "composition." The development looks random, and some of the most interesting passages appear *jeux d'esprit*. The richness of the literary art diverts attention from the substance of the argument.

But a work of art which touches on many profound problems justifies more than one kind of reading. Our difficulty with the *Phaedrus* may be that our interpretation has been too literal and too topical. If we will bring to the reading of it even a portion of that imagination which

Plato habitually exercised, we should perceive surely enough that it is consistently, and from beginning to end, about one thing, which is the nature of rhetoric.[1] Again, that point may have been missed because most readers conceive rhetoric to be a system of artifice rather than an idea,[2] and the *Phaedrus*, for all its apparent divagation, keeps very close to a single idea. A study of its rhetorical structure, especially, may give us the insight which has been withheld, while making us feel anew that Plato possessed the deepest divining rod among the ancients.

For the imaginative interpretation which we shall now undertake, we have both general and specific warrant. First, it scarcely needs pointing out that a Socratic dialogue is in itself an example of transcendence. Beginning with something simple and topical, it passes to more general levels of application; and not infrequently, it must make the leap into allegory for the final utterance. This means, of course, that a Socratic dialogue may be about its subject implicitly as well as explicitly. The implicit rendering is usually through some kind of figuration because it is the nature of this meaning to be ineffable in any other way. It is necessary, therefore, to be alert for what takes place through the analogical mode.

Second, it is a matter of curious interest that a warning against literal reading occurs at an early stage of the *Phaedrus*. Here in the opening pages, appearing as if to set the key of the theme, comes an allusion to the myth of Boreas and Oreithyia. On the very spot where the dialogue begins, Boreas is said to have carried off the maiden. Does Socrates

---

[1] Cf. A. E. Taylor, *Plato: The Man and His Work* (New York, 1936), 300.

[2] Cf. P. Albert Duhamel, "The Concept of Rhetoric as Effective Expression," *Journal of the History of Ideas*, X (June, 1949), 344–56 *passim*.

believe that this tale is really true? Or is he in favor of a scientific explanation of what the myth alleges? Athens had scientific experts, and the scientific explanation was that the north wind had pushed her off some rocks where she was playing with a companion. In this way the poetical story is provided with a factual basis. The answer of Socrates is that many tales are open to this kind of rationalization, but that the result is tedious and actually irrelevant. It is irrelevant because our chief concern is with the nature of the man, and it is beside the point to probe into such matters while we are yet ignorant of ourselves. The scientific criticism of Greek mythology, which may be likened to the scientific criticism of the myths of the Bible in our own day, produces at best "a boorish sort of wisdom ($\dot{a}\gamma\rho o\iota\kappa\omega\ \tau\iota\nu\iota\ \sigma o\phi\iota\alpha$)." It is a limitation to suppose that the truth of the story lies in its historicity. The "boorish sort of wisdom" seeks to supplant poetic allegation with fact, just as an archaeologist might look for the foundations of the Garden of Eden. But while this sort of search goes on the truth flies off, on wings of imagination, and is not recoverable until the searcher attains a higher level of pursuit. Socrates is satisfied with the parable, and we infer from numerous other passages that he believed that some things are best told by parable and some perhaps discoverable only by parable. Real investigation goes forward with the help of analogy. "Freud without Sophocles is unthinkable," a modern writer has said.[3]

With these precepts in mind, we turn to that part of the *Phaedrus* which has proved most puzzling: why is so much said about the absurd relationship of the lover and the nonlover? Socrates encounters Phaedrus outside the city

[3] James Blish, "Rituals on Ezra Pound," *Sewanee Review*, LVIII (Spring, 1950), 223.

wall. The latter has just come from hearing a discourse by Lysias which enchanted him with its eloquence. He is prevailed upon to repeat this discourse, and the two seek out a shady spot on the banks of the Ilissus. Now the discourse is remarkable because although it was "in a way, a love speech," its argument was that people should grant favors to non-lovers rather than to lovers. "This is just the clever thing about it," Phaedrus remarks. People are in the habit of preferring their lovers, but it is much more intelligent, as the argument of Lysias runs, to prefer a non-lover. Accordingly, the first major topic of the dialogue is a eulogy of the non-lover. The speech provides good subject matter for jesting on the part of Socrates, and looks like another exhibition of the childlike ingeniousness which gives the Greeks their charm. Is it merely a piece of literary trifling? Rather, it is Plato's dramatistic presentation of a major thesis. Beneath the surface of repartee and mock seriousness, he is asking whether we ought to prefer a neuter form of speech to the kind which is ever getting us aroused over things and provoking an expense of spirit.

Sophistications of theory cannot obscure the truth that there are but three ways for language to affect us. It can move us toward what is good; it can move us toward what is evil; or it can, in hypothetical third place, fail to move us at all.[4] Of course there are numberless degrees of effect under the first two heads, and the third, as will be shown, is an approximate rather than an absolute zero of effect. But any utterance is a major assumption of responsibility, and the assumption that one can avoid that responsibility by doing something to language itself is one of the chief considerations of the *Phaedrus*, just as it is of contemporary semantic

[4] The various aesthetic approaches to language offer refinements of perception, but all of them can be finally subsumed under the first head above.

theory. What Plato has succeeded in doing in this dialogue, whether by a remarkably effaced design, or unconsciously through the formal pressure of his conception, is to give us embodiments of the three types of discourse. These are respectively the non-lover, the evil lover, and the noble lover. We shall take up these figures in their sequence and show their relevance to the problem of language.

The eulogy of the non-lover in the speech of Lysias, as we hear it repeated to Socrates, stresses the fact that the non-lover follows a policy of enlightened self-interest. First of all, the non-lover does not neglect his affairs or commit extreme acts under the influence of passion. Since he acts from calculation, he never has occasion for remorse. No one ever says of him that he is not in his right mind, because all of his acts are within prudential bounds. The first point is, in sum, that the non-lover never sacrifices himself and therefore never feels the vexation which overtakes lovers when they recover from their passion and try to balance their pains with their profit. And the non-lover is constant whereas the lover is inconstant. The first argument then is that the non-lover demonstrates his superiority through prudence and objectivity. The second point of superiority found in non-lovers is that there are many more of them. If one is limited in one's choice to one's lovers, the range is small; but as there are always more non-lovers than lovers, one has a better chance in choosing among many of finding something worthy of one's affection. A third point of superiority is that association with the non-lover does not excite public comment. If one is seen going about with the object of one's love, one is likely to provoke gossip; but when one is seen conversing with the non-lover, people merely realize that "everybody must converse with somebody." Therefore this kind of relationship does not affect one's public standing, and one is not disturbed by what the neighbors are saying. Finally, non-lovers are not jealous of one's associates. Accordingly they do not try to keep one from companions of intellect or wealth for fear that they may be outshone themselves. The lover, by contrast, tries to draw his beloved away from such companionship and so deprives him of improving associations. The argument is concluded with a generalization that one ought to grant favors not to the needy or the importunate, but to those who are able to repay. Such is the favorable account of the non-lover given by Lysias.

We must now observe how these points of superiority correspond to those of "semantically purified" speech. By "semantically purified speech" we mean the kind of speech approaching pure notation in the respect that it communicates abstract intelligence without impulsion. It is a simple instrumentality, showing no affection for the object of its symbolizing and incapable of inducing bias in the hearer. In its ideal conception, it would have less power to move than $2 + 2 = 4$, since it is generally admitted that mathematical equations may have the beauty of elegance, and hence are not above suspicion where beauty is suspect. But this neuter language will be an unqualified medium of transmission of meanings from mind to mind, and by virtue of it minds can remain in an unprejudiced relationship to the world and also to other minds.

Since the characteristic of this language is absence of anything like affection, it exhibits toward the thing being represented merely a sober fidelity, like that of the non-lover toward his companion. Instead of passion, it offers the serviceability of objectivity. Its "enlightened self-interest" takes the form of an unvarying accuracy and regularity in its symbolic references, most, if not all of which will be to verifiable data in the extramental world. Like a thrifty burgher, it has no romanticism about it; and it distrusts any departure from the literal and prosaic. The burgher has his feet on the ground; and similarly the language of pure notation has its point-by-point contact with objective reality. As Stuart Chase, one of its modern proponents, says in *The Tyranny of Words*: "*If we wish to understand the world and ourselves, it follows that we should use a language whose structure corresponds to physical structure*"[5] (italics his). So this language is married to the world, and its marital fidelity contrasts with the extravagances of other languages.

In second place, this language is far more "available." Whereas rhetorical language, or language which would persuade, must always be particularized to suit the occasion, drawing its effectiveness from many small nuances, a "utility" language is very general and one has no difficulty putting his meaning into it if he is satisfied with a paraphrase of that meaning. The 850 words recommended for Basic English, for example, are highly available in the sense that all native users of English have them instantly ready and learners of English can quickly acquire them. It soon becomes apparent, however, that the availability is a heavy tax upon all other qualities. Most of what we admire as energy and fullness tends to disappear when mere verbal counters are used. The conventional or public aspect of

[5] *The Tyranny of Words* (New York, 1938), 80. T. H. Huxley in *Lay Sermons* (New York, 1883), 112, outlined a noticeably similar ideal of scientific communication: "Therefore, the great business of the scientific teacher is, to imprint the fundamental, irrefragable facts of his science, not only by words upon the mind, but by sensible impressions upon the eye, and ear, and touch of the student in so complete a manner, that every term used, or law enunciated should afterwards call up vivid images of the particular structural, or other, facts which furnished the demonstration of the law, or illustration of the term."

language can encroach upon the suggestive or symbolical aspect, until the naming is vague or blurred. In proportion as the medium is conventional in the widest sense and avoids all individualizing, personalizing, and heightening terms, it is common, and the commonness constitutes the negative virtue ascribed to the non-lover.

Finally, with reference to the third qualification of the non-lover, it is true that neuter language does not excite public opinion. This fact follows from its character outlined above. Rhetorical language on the other hand, for whatever purpose used, excites interest and with it either pleasure or alarm. People listen instinctively to the man whose speech betrays inclination. It does not matter what the inclination is toward, but we may say that the greater the degree of inclination, the greater the curiosity or response. Hence a "style" in speech always causes one to be a marked man, and the public may not be so much impressed—at least initially—by what the man is for or against as by the fact that he has a style. The way therefore to avoid public comment is to avoid the speech of affection and to use that of business, since, to echo the original proposition of Lysias, everybody knows that one must do business with others. From another standpoint, then, this is the language of prudence. These are the features which give neuter discourse an appeal to those who expect a scientific solution of human problems.

In summing up the trend of meaning, we note that Lysias has been praising a disinterested kind of relationship which avoids all excesses and irrationalities, all the dementia of love. It is a circumspect kind of relationship, which is preferred by all men who wish to do well in the world and avoid tempestuous courses. We have compared its detachment with the kind of abstraction to be found in scientific notation. But as an earnest of what is to come let us note, in taking leave of this part, that Phaedrus expresses admiration for the eloquence, especially of diction, with which the suit of the non-lover has been urged. This is our warning of the dilemma of the non-lover.

Now we turn to the second major speech of the dialogue, which is made by Socrates. Notwithstanding Phaedrus' enthusiastic praise, Socrates is dissatisfied with the speech of the non-lover. He remembers having heard wiser things on the subject and feels that he can make a speech on the same theme "different from this and quite as good." After some playful exchange, Socrates launches upon his own abuse of love, which centers on the point that the lover is an exploiter. Love (ἔρως) is defined as the kind of desire which overcomes rational opinion and moves toward the enjoyment of personal or bodily beauty. The lover wishes to make the object of his passion as pleasing to himself as possible; but to those possessed by this frenzy, only that which is subject to their will is pleasant. Accordingly, everything which is opposed, or is equal or better, the lover views with hostility. He naturally therefore tries to make the beloved inferior to himself in every respect. He is pleased if the beloved has intellectual limitations because they have the effect of making him manageable. For a similar reason he tries to keep him away from all influences which might "make a man of him," and of course the greatest of these is divine philosophy. While he is working to keep him intellectually immature, he works also to keep him weak and effeminate, with such harmful result that the beloved is unable to play a man's part in crises. The lover is, moreover, jealous of the possession of property because this gives the beloved an independence which he does not wish him to have. Thus the lover in exercising an unremitting compulsion over the beloved deprives him of all praiseworthy qualities, and this is the price the beloved pays for accepting a lover who is "necessarily without reason." In brief, the lover is not motivated by benevolence toward the beloved, but by selfish appetite; and Socrates can aptly close with the quotation: "As wolves love lambs, so lovers love their loves." The speech is on the single theme of exploitation. It is important for us to keep in mind the object of love as here described, because another kind of love with a different object is later introduced into the dialogue, and we shall discuss the counterpart of each.

As we look now for the parallel in language, we find ourselves confronting the second of the three alternatives: speech which influences us in the direction of what is evil. This we shall call base rhetoric because its end is the exploitation which Socrates has been condemning. We find that base rhetoric hates that which is opposed, or is equal or better because all such things are impediments to its will, and in the last analysis it knows only its will. Truth is the stubborn, objective restraint which this will endeavors to overcome. Base rhetoric is therefore always trying to keep its objects from the support which personal courage, noble associations, and divine philosophy provide a man.

The base rhetorician, we may say, is a man who has yielded to the wrong aspects of existence. He has allowed himself to succumb to the sights and shows, to the physical pleasures which conspire against noble life. He knows that the only way he can get a following in his pursuits (and a following seems necessary to maximum enjoyment of the pursuits) is to work against the true understanding of his followers. Consequently the things which would elevate he keeps out of sight, and the things with which he surrounds his "beloved" are those which minister immediately to desire. The beloved is thus emasculated in understanding in order that the lover may have his way. Or as Socrates expresses it, the selfish lover contrives things so that the beloved will be "most agreeable to him and most harmful to himself."

Examples of this kind of contrivance occur on every hand in the impassioned language of journalism and political pleading. In the world of affairs which these seek to influence, the many are kept in a state of pupillage so that they will be most docile to their "lovers." The techniques of the base lover, especially as exemplified in modern journalism, would make a long catalogue, but in general it is accurate to say that he seeks to keep the understanding in a passive state by never permitting an honest examination of alternatives. Nothing is more feared by him than a true dialectic, for this not only endangers his favored alternative, but also gives the "beloved"—how clearly here are these the "lambs" of Socrates' figure—some training in intellectual independence. What he does therefore is dress up one alternative in all the cheap finery of immediate hopes and fears, knowing that if he can thus prevent a masculine exercise of imagination and will, he can have his way. By discussing only one side of an issue, by mentioning cause without consequence or consequence without cause, acts without agents or agents without agency,[6] he often successfully blocks definition and cause-and-effect reasoning. In this way his choices are arrayed in such meretricious images that one can quickly infer the juvenile mind which they would attract. Of course the base rhetorician today, with his vastly augmented power of propagation, has means of deluding which no ancient rhetor in forum or market place could have imagined.

[6] That is, by mentioning only parts of the total situation.

Because Socrates has now made a speech against love, representing it as an evil, the non-lover seems to survive in estimation. We observe, however, that the non-lover, instead of being celebrated, is disposed of dialectically. "So, in a word, I say that the non-lover possesses all the advantages that are opposed to the disadvantages we found in the lover." This is not without bearing upon the subject matter of the important third speech, to which we now turn.

At this point in the dialogue, Socrates is warned by his monitory spirit that he has been engaging in a defamation of love despite the fact that love is a divinity. "If love is, as indeed he is, a god or something divine, he can be nothing evil; but the two speeches just now said that he was evil." These discourses were then an impiety—one representing non-love as admirable and the other attacking love as base. Socrates resolves to make amends, and the recantation which follows is one of the most elaborate developments in the Platonic system. The account of love which emerges from this new position may be summarized as follows.

Love is often censured as a form of madness, yet not all madness is evil. There is a madness which is simple degeneracy, but on the other hand there are kinds of madness which are really forms of inspiration, from which come the greatest gifts conferred on man. Prophecy is a kind of madness, and so too is poetry. "The poetry of the sane man vanishes into nothingness before that of the inspired madman." Mere sanity, which is of human origin, is inferior to that madness which is inspired by the gods and which is a condition for the highest kind of achievement. In this category goes the madness of the true lover. His is a generous state which confers blessings to the ignoring of self, whereas the conduct of the non-lover displays all the selfishness of business: "the affection of the non-lover, which is alloyed with mortal prudence and follows mortal and parsimonious rules of conduct will beget in the beloved soul the narrowness which common folk praise as virtue; it will cause the soul to be a wanderer upon the earth for nine thousand years and a fool below the earth at last." It is the vulgar who do not realize that the madness of the noble lover is an inspired madness because he has his thoughts turned toward a beauty of divine origin.

Now the attitude of the noble lover toward the beloved is in direct contrast with that of the evil lover, who, as we have seen, strives to possess and victimize the object of his affections. For once the noble lover has mastered the conflict within his own soul by conquering appetite and fixing his attention upon the intelligible and the divine, he conceives an exalted attitude toward the beloved. The noble lover now "follows the beloved in reverence and awe." So those who are filled with this kind of love "exhibit no jealousy or meanness toward the loved one, but endeavor by every means in their power to lead him to the likeness of the god whom they honor." Such is the conversion by which love turns from the exploitative to the creative.

Here it becomes necessary to bring our concepts together and to think of all speech having persuasive power as a kind of "love."[7] Thus, rhetorical speech is madness to the extent that it departs from the line which mere sanity lays down. There is always in its statement a kind of excess or deficiency which is immediately discernible when the test of simple realism is applied. Simple realism operates on a principle of equation or correspondence; one thing must match another, or, representation must tally with thing

[7] It is worth recalling that in the Christian New Testament, with its heavy Platonic influence, God is identified both with *logos*, "word, speech" (John 1:1); and with *agape*, "love" (2 John 4:8).

represented, like items in a tradesman's account. Any excess
or deficiency on the part of the representation invokes the
existence of the world of symbolism, which simple realism
must deny. This explains why there is an immortal feud
between men of business and the users of metaphor and
metonymy, the poets and the rhetoricians.[8] The man of
business, the narrow and parsimonious soul in the allusion
of Socrates, desires a world which is a reliable materiality.
But this the poet and rhetorician will never let him have,
for each, with his own purpose, is trying to advance the
borders of the imaginative world. A primrose by the river's
brim will not remain that in the poet's account, but is
promptly turned into something very much larger and
something highly implicative. He who is accustomed to
record the world with an abacus cannot follow these trans-
figurations; and indeed the very occurrence of them subtly
undermines the premise of his business. It is the historic
tendency of the tradesman, therefore, to confine passion to
quite narrow channels so that it will not upset the decent
business arrangements of the world. But if the poet, as the
chief transformer of our picture of the world, is the peculiar
enemy of this mentality, the rhetorician is also hostile
when practicing the kind of love proper to him. The "passion" in his speech is revolutionary, and it has a practical
end.

We have now indicated the significance of the three
types of lovers; but the remainder of the *Phaedrus* has
much more to say about the nature of rhetoric, and we
must return to one or more points to place our subject in a
wider context. The problem of rhetoric which occupied
Plato persistently, not only in the *Phaedrus* but also in

---

[8] The users of metaphor and metonymy who are in the hire of business-
men of course constitute a special case.

other dialogues where this art is reviewed, may be best stated as a question: if truth alone is not sufficient to persuade men, what else remains that can be legitimately added? In one of the exchanges with Phaedrus, Socrates puts the question in the mouth of a personified Rhetoric: "I do not compel anyone to learn to speak without knowing the truth, but if my advice is of any value, he learns that first and then acquires me. So what I claim is this, that without my help the knowledge of the truth does not give the art of persuasion."

Now rhetoric as we have discussed it in relation to the lovers consists of truth plus its artful presentation, and for this reason it becomes necessary to say something more about the natural order of dialectic and rhetoric. In any general characterization rhetoric will include dialectic,[9] but for the study of method it is necessary to separate the two. Dialectic is a method of investigation whose object is the establishment of truth about doubtful propositions. Aristotle in the *Topics* gives a concise statement of its nature. "A dialectical problem is a subject of inquiry that contributes either to choice or avoidance, or to truth and knowledge, and that either by itself, or as a help to the solution of some other such problem. It must, moreover, be something on which either people hold no opinion either way, or the masses hold a contrary opinion to the philosophers, or the philosophers to the masses, or each of them among them-

---

[9] Cf. 227b: "A man must know the truth about all the particular things of which he speaks or writes, and must be able to define everything separately; then when he has defined them, he must know how to divide them by classes until further division is impossible; and in the same way he must understand the nature of the soul, must find out the class of speech adapted to each nature, and must arrange and adorn his discourse accordingly, offering to the complex soul eleborate and harmonious discourses, and simple talks to the simple soul."

selves."[10] Plato is not perfectly clear about the distinction between positive and dialectical terms. In one passage[11] he contrasts the "positive" terms "iron" and "silver" with the "dialectical" terms "justice" and "goodness"; yet in other passages his "dialectical" terms seem to include categorizations of the external world. Thus Socrates indicates that distinguishing the horse from the ass is a dialectical operation;[12] and he tells us later that a good dialectician is able to divide things by classes "where the natural joints are" and will avoid breaking any part "after the manner of a bad carver."[13] Such, perhaps, is Aristotle's dialectic which contributes to truth and knowledge.

But there is a branch of dialectic which contributes to "choice or avoidance," and it is with this that rhetoric is regularly found joined. Generally speaking, this is a rhetoric involving questions of policy, and the dialectic which precedes it will determine not the application of positive terms but that of terms which are subject to the contingency of evaluation. Here dialectical inquiry will concern itself not with what is "iron" but with what is "good." It seeks to establish what belongs in the category of the "just" rather than what belongs in the genus *Canis*. As a general rule, simple object words such as "iron" and "house" have no connotations of policy, although it is frequently possible to give them these through speech situations in which there is added to their referential function a kind of impulse. We should have to interpret in this way "Fire!" or "Gold!" because these terms acquire something through intonation and relationship which places them in the class of evaluative expressions.

[10] 104b.
[11] 263a.
[12] 260b.
[13] 265a.

Any piece of persuasion, therefore, will contain as its first process a dialectic establishing terms which have to do with policy. Now a term of policy is essentially a term of motion, and here begins the congruence of rhetoric with the soul which underlies the speculation of the *Phaedrus*. In his myth of the charioteer, Socrates declares that every soul is immortal because "that which is ever moving is immortal." Motion, it would appear from this definition, is part of the soul's essence. And just because the soul is ever tending, positive or indifferent terms cannot partake of this congruence. But terms of tendency—goodness, justice, divinity, and the like—are terms of motion and therefore may be said to comport with the soul's essence. The soul's perception of goodness, justice, and divinity will depend upon its proper tendency, while at the same time contacts with these in discourse confirm and direct that tendency. The education of the soul is not a process of bringing it into correspondence with a physical structure like the external world, but rather a process of rightly affecting its motion. By this conception, a soul which is rightly affected calls that good which is good; but a soul which is wrongly turned calls that good which is evil. What Plato has prepared us to see is that the virtuous rhetorician, who is a lover of truth, has a soul of such movement that its dialectical perceptions are consonant with those of a divine mind. Or, in the language of more technical philosophy, this soul is aware of axiological systems which have ontic status. The good soul, consequently, will not urge a perversion of justice as justice in order to impose upon the commonwealth. Insofar as the soul has its impulse in the right direction, its definitions will agree with the true nature of intelligible things.

There is, then, no true rhetoric without dialectic, for the dialectic provides that basis of "high speculation about nature" without which rhetoric in the narrower sense has nothing to work upon. Yet, when the disputed terms have been established, we are at the limit of dialectic. How does the noble rhetorician proceed from this point on? That the clearest demonstration in terms of logical inclusion and exclusion often fails to win assent we hardly need state; therefore, to what does the rhetorician resort at this critical passage? It is the stage at which he passes from the logical to the analogical, or it is where figuration comes into rhetoric.

To look at this for a moment through a practical illustration, let us suppose that a speaker has convinced his listeners that his position is "true" as far as dialectical inquiry may be pushed. Now he sets about moving the listeners toward that position, but there is no way to move them except through the operation of analogy. The analogy proceeds by showing that the position being urged resembles or partakes of something greater and finer. It will be represented, in sum, as one of the steps leading toward ultimate good. Let us further suppose our speaker to be arguing for the payment of a just debt. The payment of the just debt is not itself justice, but the payment of this particular debt is one of the many things which would have to be done before this could be a completely just world. It is just, then, because it partakes of the ideal justice, or it is a small analogue of all justice (in practice it will be found that the rhetorician makes extensive use of synecdoche, whereby the small part is used as a vivid suggestion of the grandeur of the whole). It is by bringing out these resemblances ·that the good rhetorician leads those who listen in the direction of what is good. In effect, he performs a cure of souls by giving impulse, chiefly through figuration, toward an ideal good.

We now see the true rhetorician as a noble lover of the

good, who works through dialectic and through poetic or analogical association. However he is compelled to modulate by the peculiar features of an occasion, this is his method.

It may not be superfluous to draw attention to the fact that what we have here outlined is the method of the *Phaedrus* itself. The dialectic appears in the dispute about love. The current thesis that love is praiseworthy is countered by the antithesis that love is blameworthy. This position is fully developed in the speech of Lysias and in the first speech of Socrates. But this position is countered by a new thesis that after all love is praiseworthy because it is a divine thing. Of course, this is love on a higher level, or love re-defined. This is the regular process of transcendence which we have noted before. Now, having rescued love from the imputation of evil by excluding certain things from its definition, what does Socrates do? Quite in accordance with our analysis, he turns rhetorician. He tries to make this love as attractive as possible by bringing in the splendid figure of the charioteer.[14] In the narrower conception of this art, the allegory is the rhetoric, for it excites and fills us with desire for this kind of love, depicted with many terms having tendency toward the good. But in the broader conception the art must include also the dialectic, which succeeded in placing love in the category of divine things before filling our imaginations with attributes of divinity.[15] It is so regularly the method of Plato to follow a subtle analysis with a striking myth that it is not unreasonable to call him the master rhetorician. This goes far to explain why those who reject his philosophy sometimes remark his literary art with mingled admiration and annoyance.

[14] In the passage extending from 246a to 256d.
[15] Cf. 263d ff.

The objection sometimes made that rhetoric cannot be used by a lover of truth because it indulges in "exaggerations" can be answered as follows. There is an exaggeration which is mere wantonness, and with this the true rhetorician has nothing to do. Such exaggeration is purely impressionistic in aim. Like caricature, whose only object is to amuse, it seizes upon any trait or aspect which could produce titillation and exploits this without conscience. If all rhetoric were like this, we should have to grant that rhetoricians are persons of very low responsibility and their art a disreputable one. But the rhetorician we have now defined is not interested in sensationalism.

The exaggeration which this rhetorician employs is not caricature but prophecy; and it would be a fair formulation to say that true rhetoric is concerned with the potency of things. The literalist, like the anti-poet described earlier, is troubled by its failure to conform to a present reality. What he fails to appreciate is that potentiality is a mode of existence, and that all prophecy is about the tendency of things. The discourse of the noble rhetorician, accordingly, will be about real potentiality or possible actuality, whereas that of the mere exaggerator is about unreal potentiality. Naturally this distinction rests upon a supposal that the rhetorician has insight, and we could not defend him in the absence of that condition. But given insight, he has the duty to represent to us the as yet unactualized future. It would be, for example, a misrepresentation of current facts but not of potential ones to talk about the joys of peace in a time of war. During the Second World War, at the depth of Britain's political and military disaster, Winston Churchill likened the future of Europe to "broad sunlit uplands." Now if one had regard only for the hour, this was a piece of mendacity such as the worst charlatans are found committing; but if one took Churchill's premises and then considered the potentiality, the picture was within bounds of actualization. His "exaggeration" was that the defeat of the enemy would place Europe in a position for long and peaceful progress. At the time the surface trends ran the other way; the actuality was a valley of humiliation. Yet the hope which transfigured this to "broad sunlit uplands" was not irresponsible, and we conclude by saying that the rhetorician talks about both what exists simply and what exists by favor of human imagination and effort.[16]

This interest in actualization is a further distinction between pure dialectic and rhetoric. With its forecast of the actual possibility, rhetoric passes from mere scientific demonstration of an idea to its relation to prudential conduct. A dialectic must take place *in vacuo*, and the fact alone that it contains contraries leaves it an intellectual thing. Rhetoric, on the other hand, always espouses one of the contraries. This espousal is followed by some attempt at impingement upon actuality. That is why rhetoric, with its passion for the actual, is more complete than mere dialectic with its dry understanding. It is more complete on the premise that man is a creature of passion who must live

[16] Indeed, in this particular rhetorical duel we see the two types of lovers opposed as clearly as illustration could desire. More than this, we see the third type, the non-lover, commiting his ignominious failure. Britain and France had come to prefer as leaders the rhetoricless businessman type. And while they had thus emasculated themselves, there appeared an evil lover to whom Europe all but succumbed before the mistake was seen and rectified. For while the world must move, evil rhetoric is of more force than no rhetoric at all; and Herr Hitler, employing images which rested on no true dialectic, had persuaded multitudes that his order was the "new order," i.e., the true potentiality. Britain was losing and could only lose until, reaching back in her traditional past, she found a voice which could match his accents with a truer grasp of the potentiality of things. Thus two men conspicuous for passion fought a contest for souls, which the nobler won. But the contest could have been lost by default.

out that passion in the world. Pure contemplation does not suffice for this end. As Jacques Maritain has expressed it: "love . . . is not directed at possibilities or pure essences; it is directed at what exists; one does not love possibilities, one loves that which exists or is destined to exist."[17] The complete man, then, is the "lover" added to the scientist; the rhetorician to the dialectician. Understanding followed by actualization seems to be the order of creation, and there is no need for the role of rhetoric to be misconceived.

The pure dialectician is left in the theoretical position of the non-lover, who can attain understanding but who cannot add impulse to truth. We are compelled to say "theoretical position" because it is by no means certain that in the world of actual speech the non-lover has more than a putative existence. We have seen previously that his speech would consist of strictly referential words which would serve only as designata. Now the question arises at what point is motive to come into such language? Kenneth Burke in A *Grammar of Motives* has pointed to "the pattern of embarrassment behind the contemporary ideal of a language that will best promote good action by entirely eliminating the element of exhortation or command. Insofar as such a project succeeded, its terms would involve a narrowing of circumference to a point where the principle of personal action is eliminated from language, so that an act would follow from it only as a non sequitur, a kind of humanitarian after-thought."[18]

The fault of this conception of language is that scientific intention turns out to be enclosed in artistic intention and not *vice versa*. Let us test this by taking as an example one of those "fact-finding committees" so favored by modern

---

[17] "Action: The Perfection of Human Life," *Sewanee Review*, LVI (Winter, 1948), 3.
[18] A *Grammar of Motives* (New York, 1945), 90.

representative governments. A language in which all else is suppressed in favor of nuclear meanings would be an ideal instrumentality for the report of such a committee. But this committee, if it lived up to the ideal of its conception, would have to be followed by an "attitude-finding committee" to tell us what its explorations really mean. In real practice the fact-finding committee understands well enough that it is also an attitude-finding committee, and where it cannot show inclination through language of tendency, it usually manages to do so through selection and arrangement of the otherwise inarticulate facts. To recur here to the original situation in the dialogue, we recall that the eloquent Lysias, posing as a non-lover, had concealed designs upon Phaedrus, so that his fine speech was really a sheep's clothing. Socrates discerned in him a "peculiar craftiness." One must suspect the same today of many who ask us to place our faith in the neutrality of their discourse. We cannot deny that there are degrees of objectivity in the reference of speech. But this is not the same as an assurance that a vocabulary of reduced meanings will solve the problems of mankind. Many of those problems will have to be handled, as Socrates well knew, by the student of souls, who must primarily make use of the language of tendency. The soul is impulse, not simply cognition; and finally one's interest in rhetoric depends on how much poignancy one senses in existence.[19]

[19] Without rhetoric there seems no possibility of tragedy, and in turn, without the sense of tragedy, no possibility of taking an elevated view of life. The role of tragedy is to keep the human lot from being rendered as history. The cultivation of tragedy and a deep interest in the value-conferring power of language always occur together. The *Phaedrus*, the *Gorgias*, and the *Cratylus*, not to mention the works of many teachers of rhetoric, appear at the close of the great age of Greek tragedy. The Elizabethan age teemed with treatises on the use of language. The essentially tragic Christian view of life begins the long tradition of homiletics. Tragedy and the practice of rhetoric seem to find common sustenance in preoccupation with value, and then rhetoric follows as an analyzed art.

Rhetoric moves the soul with a movement which cannot finally be justified logically. It can only be valued analogically with reference to some supreme image. Therefore when the rhetorician encounters some soul "sinking beneath the double load of forgetfulness and vice" he seeks to re-animate it by holding up to its sight the order of presumptive goods. This order is necessarily a hierarchy leading up to the ultimate good. All of the terms in a rhetorical vocabulary are like links in a chain stretching up to some master link which transmits its influence down through the linkages. It is impossible to talk about rhetoric as effective expression without having as a term giving intelligibility to the whole discourse, the Good. Of course, inferior concepts of the Good may be and often are placed in this ultimate position; and there is nothing to keep a base lover from inverting the proper order and saying, "Evil, be thou my good." Yet the fact remains that in any piece of rhetorical discourse, one rhetorical term overcomes another rhetorical term only by being nearer to the term which stands ultimate. There is some ground for calling a rhetorical education necessarily an aristocratic education in that the rhetorician has to deal with an aristocracy of notions, to say nothing of supplementing his logical and pathetic proofs with an ethical proof.

All things considered, rhetoric, noble or base, is a great power in the world; and we note accordingly that at the center of the public life of every people there is a fierce struggle over who shall control the means of rhetorical propagation. Today we set up "offices of information," which like the sly lover in the dialogue, pose as non-lovers while pushing their suits. But there is no reason to despair over the fact that men will never give up seeking to influence one another. We would not desire it to be otherwise;

neuter discourse is a false idol, to worship which is to commit the very offense for which Socrates made expiation in his second speech.

Since we want not emancipation from impulse but clarification of impulse, the duty of rhetoric is to bring together action and understanding into a whole that is greater than scientific perception.[20] The realization that just as no action is really indifferent, so no utterance is without its responsibility introduces, it is true, a certain strenuosity into life, produced by a consciousness that "nothing is lost." Yet this is preferable to that desolation which proceeds from an infinite dispersion or feeling of unaccountability. Even so, the choice between them is hardly ours to make; we did not create the order of things, but being accountable for our impulses, we wish these to be just.

Thus when we finally divest rhetoric of all the notions of artifice which have grown up around it, we are left with something very much like Spinoza's "intellectual love of God." This is its essence and the *fons et origo* of its power. It is "intellectual" because, as we have previously seen, there is no honest rhetoric without a preceding dialectic. The kind of rhetoric which is justly condemned is utter-

---

[20] Cf. Maritain, *op. cit.*, 3–4: "The truth of practical intellect is understood not as conformity to an extramental being but as conformity to a right desire; the end is no longer to know what is, but to bring into existence that which is not yet; further, the act of moral choice is so individualized, both by the singularity of the person from which it proceeds and the context of the contingent circumstances in which it takes place, that the practical judgment in which it is expressed and by which I declare to myself: this is what I must do, can be right only if, *hic et nunc*, the dynamism of my will is right, and tends towards the true goods of human life.

That is why practical wisdom, *prudentia*, is a virtue indivisibly moral and intellectual at the same time, and why, like the judgement of the conscience itself, it cannot be replaced by any sort of theoretical knowledge or science."

ance in support of a position before that position has been adjudicated with reference to the whole universe of discourse[21]—and of such the world always produces more than enough. It is "love" because it is something in addition to bare theoretical truth. That element in addition is a desire to bring truth into a kind of existence, or to give it an actuality to which theory is indifferent. Now what is to be said about our last expression, "of God"? Echoes of theological warfare will cause many to desire a substitute for this, and we should not object. As long as we have in ultimate place the highest good man can intuit, the relationship is made perfect. We shall be content with "intellectual love of the Good." It is still the intellectual love of good which causes the noble lover to desire not to devour his beloved but to shape him according to the gods as far as mortal power allows. So rhetoric at its truest seeks to perfect men by showing them better versions of themselves, links in that chain extending up toward the ideal, which only the intellect can apprehend and only the soul have affection for. This is the justified affection of which no one can be ashamed, and he who feels no influence of it is truly outside the communion of minds. Rhetoric appears, finally, as a means by which the impulse of the soul to be ever moving is redeemed.

It may be granted that in this essay we have gone some distance from the banks of the Ilissus. What began as a simple account of passion becomes by transcendence an allegory of all speech. No one would think of suggesting that Plato had in mind every application which has here been made, but that need not arise as an issue. The struc-

---

[21] Socrates' criticism of the speech of Lysias (263d ff) is that the latter defended a position without having submitted it to the discipline of dialectic.

ture of the dialogue, the way in which the judgments about speech concentre, and especially the close association of the true, the beautiful, and the good, constitute a unity of implication. The central idea is that all speech, which is the means the gods have given man to express his soul, is a form of eros, in the proper interpretation of the word. With that truth the rhetorician will always be brought face to face as soon as he ventures beyond the consideration of mere artifice and device.

I tend to part company [with you], however, at the point [in your essay] where you hitch rhetoric to democracy. . . . It [democracy] is something that has virtues and limitations, and I think it is very dubious to set it up as a be-all, end-all. . . . My point is that I cannot see democracy as the object of all rhetorical endeavor . . . . To do so subjects rhetoric to something that is an instrument itself, and I see rhetoric as serving the highest goals of human life, which are expressible only through the profounder ideas of freedom, justice, and order. Please do not draw the conclusion that I am a royalist, or something like that. What I am really objecting to here is a kind of canonization of democracy which actually does it more harm than good and may indeed eventually lead to the loss of it by confusing it with things it is not. I would settle for treating the matter in greater perspective—that is—tieing democracy to certain ideals of value which are themselves the ultimate goals.

—Richard M. Weaver to Ralph T. Eubanks
January 19, 1961

Central to Weaver's philosophy of rhetoric was the idea of a proper ordering of the goods. Thus, one of the core functions of dialectic is to enable man to order and to appraise his terms. There is, Weaver believed, a hierarchy of terms capable of moving man to action. In the essay that follows, Weaver explores rhetorical practices with emphasis upon the emergence of values in the "god terms" and "charismatic terms" of our age. Written as the last chapter for *The Ethics of Rhetoric,* "Ultimate Terms" is Weaver's attempt "to make an empirical study of . . . terms" in their contemporary setting. From this analysis emerges Weaver's plea that the major goal of an ethical rhetoric must be to keep "ultimate terms . . . ultimate in a rational sense."

Ultimate Terms
in Contemporary Rhetoric

We have shown that rhetorical force must be conceived as a power transmitted through the links of a chain that extends upward toward some ultimate source. The higher links of that chain must always be of unique interest to the student of rhetoric, pointing, as they do, to some prime mover of human impulse. Here I propose to turn away from general considerations and to make an empirical study of the terms on these higher levels of force which are seen to be operating in our age.

We shall define term simply here as a name capable of entering into a proposition. In our treatment of rhetorical sources, we have regarded the full predication consisting of a proposition as the true validator. But a single term is an incipient proposition, awaiting only the necessary coupling with another term; and it cannot be denied that single names set up expectancies of propositional embodiment. This causes everyone to realize the critical nature of the process of naming. Given the name "patriot," for example, we might expect to see coupled with it "Brutus," or "Washington," or "Parnell"; given the term "hot," we might expect to see "sun," "stove," and so on. In sum, single terms have their potencies, this being part of the phenomenon of names, and we shall here present a few of the most noteworthy in our time, with some remarks upon their etiology.

Naturally this survey will include the "bad" terms as well as the "good" terms, since we are interested to record historically those expressions to which the populace, in its actual usage and response, appears to attribute the greatest sanction. A prescriptive rhetoric may specify those terms which, in all seasons, ought to carry the greatest potency, but since the affections of one age are frequently a source of wonder to another, the most we can do under the caption "contemporary rhetoric" is to give a descriptive account and withhold the moral until the end. For despite the variations of fashion, an age which is not simply distraught manages to achieve some system of relationship among the attractive and among the repulsive terms, so that we can work out an order of weight and precedence in the prevailing rhetoric once we have discerned the "rhetorical absolutes"—the terms to which the very highest respect is paid.

It is best to begin boldly by asking ourselves, what is the "god term" of the present age? By "god term" we mean that expression about which all other expressions are ranked as subordinate and serving dominations and powers. Its force imparts to the others their lesser degree of force, and fixes the scale by which degrees of comparison are understood. In the absence of a strong and evenly diffused religion, there may be several terms competing for this primacy, so that the question is not always capable of definite answer. Yet if one has to select the one term which in our day carries the greatest blessing, and—to apply a useful test—whose antonym carries the greatest rebuke, one will not go far wrong in naming "progress." This seems to be the ultimate generator of force flowing down through many links of ancillary terms. If one can "make it stick," it will validate almost anything. It would be difficult to think of any type of person or of any institution which could not be recommended to the public through the enhancing power of this word. A politician is urged upon the voters as a "progressive leader"; a community is proud to style itself "progressive"; technologies and methodologies claim to the "progressive"; a peculiar kind of emphasis in modern education calls itself "progressive;" and so on without limit. There is no word whose power to move is more implicitly trusted than "progressive." But unlike some other words we shall examine in the course of this chapter, its rise to supreme position is not obscure, and it possesses some intelligible referents.

Before going into the story of its elevation, we must prepare ground by noting that it is the nature of the conscious life of man to revolve around some concept of value. So true is this that when the concept is withdrawn, or when it is forced into competition with another concept, the human being suffers an almost intolerable sense of being lost. He has to know where he is in the ideological cosmos in order to coordinate his activities. Probably the greatest cruelty which can be inflicted upon the psychic man is this deprivation of a sense of tendency. Accordingly every age, including those of rudest cultivation, sets up some kind of sign post. In highly cultivated ages, with individuals of exceptional intellectual strength, this may take the form of a metaphysic. But with the ordinary man, even in such advanced ages, it is likely to be some idea abstracted from religion or historical speculation, and made to inhere in a few sensible and immediate examples.

Since the sixteenth century we have tended to accept as inevitable an historical development that takes the form of a changing relationship between ourselves and nature, in which we pass increasingly into the role of master of nature. When I say that this seems inevitable to us, I mean that it seems something so close to what our more religious forebears considered the working of providence that we regard as impiety any disposition to challenge or even suspect it. By a transposition of terms, "progress" becomes the salvation man is placed on earth to work out; and just as there can be no achievement more important than salvation, so there can be no activity more justified in enlisting our sympathy and support than "progress." As our historical sketch would imply, the term began to be used in the sixteenth century in the sense of continuous development or improvement; it reached an apogee in the nineteenth century, amid noisy demonstrations of man's mastery of nature, and now in the twentieth century it keeps its place as one of the least assailable of the "uncontested terms," despite critical doubts in certain philosophic quarters. It is probably the only term which gives to the average American or West European of today a concept of something bigger than himself, which he is socially impelled to accept and even to sacrifice for. This capacity to demand sacrifice is probably the surest indicator of the "god term," for when a term is so sacrosanct that the material goods of this life must be mysteriously rendered up for it, then we feel justified in saying that it is in some sense ultimate. Today no one is startled to hear of a man's sacrificing health or wealth for the "progress" of the community, whereas such sacrifices for other ends may be regarded as self-indulgent or even treasonable. And this is just because "progress" is the coordinator of all socially respectable effort.

Perhaps these observations will help the speaker who would speak against the stream of "progress," or who, on the other hand, would parry some blow aimed at him through the potency of the word, to realize what a momentum he is opposing.

Another word of great rhetorical force which owes its origin to the same historical transformation is "fact." Today's speaker says "It is a fact" with all the gravity and air of finality with which his less secular-minded ancestor would have said "It is the truth."[1] "These are facts"; "Facts tend to show"; and "He knows the facts" will be recognized as common locutions drawing upon the rhetorical resource of this word. The word "fact" went into the ascendent when our system of verification changed during the Renaissance. Prior to that time, the type of conclusion that men felt obligated to accept came either through divine revelation, or through dialectic, which obeys logical law. But these were displaced by the system of verification through correspondence with physical reality. Since then things have been true only when measurably true, or when susceptible to some kind of quantification. Quite simply, "fact" came to be the touchstone after the truth of speculative inquiry had been replaced by the truth of empirical investigation. Today when the average citizen says "It is a fact" or says that he "knows the facts in the case," he means that he has the kind of knowledge to which all other knowledges must defer. Possibly it should be pointed out that his "facts" are frequently not facts at all in the etymo-

[1] It is surely worth observing that nowhere in the King James Version of the Bible does the word "fact" occur.

logical sense; often they will be deductions several steps removed from simply factual data. Yet the "facts" of his case carry with them this aura of scientific irrefragability, and he will likely regard any questioning of them as sophistry. In his vocabulary a fact is a fact, and all evidence so denominated has the prestige of science.

These last remarks will remind us at once of the strongly rhetorical character of the word "science" itself. If there is good reason for placing "progress" rather than "science" at the top of our series, it is only that the former has more scope, "science" being the methodological tool of "progress." It seems clear, moreover, that "science" owes its present status to an hypostatization. The hypostatized term is one which treats as a substance or a concrete reality that which has only conceptual existence; and every reader will be able to supply numberless illustrations of how "science" is used without any specific referent. Any utterance beginning "Science says" provides one: "Science says there is no difference in brain capacity between the races"; "Science now knows the cause of encephalitis"; "Science says that smoking does not harm the throat." Science is not, as here it would seem to be, a single concrete entity speaking with one authoritative voice. Behind these large abstractions (and this is not an argument against abstractions as such) there are many scientists holding many different theories and employing many different methods of investigation. The whole force of the word nevertheless depends upon a bland assumption that all scientists meet periodically in synod and there decide and publish what science believes. Yet anyone with the slightest scientific training knows that this is very far from a possibility. Let us consider therefore the changed quality of the utterance when it is amended to read "A majority of scientists say"; or "Many scientists believe"; or "Some scientific experiments have indicated." The change will not do. There has to be a creature called "science"; and its creation has as a matter of practice been easy, because modern man has been conditioned to believe that the powers and processes which have transformed his material world represent a very sure form of knowledge, and that there must be a way of identifying that knowledge. Obviously the rhetorical aggrandizement of "science" here parallels that of "fact," the one representing generally and the other specifically the whole subject matter of trustworthy perception.

Furthermore, the term "science" like "progress" seems to satisfy a primal need. Man feels lost without a touchstone of knowledge just as he feels lost without the direction-finder provided by progress. It is curious to note that actually the word is only another name for knowledge (L. *scientia*), so that if we should go by strict etymology, we should insist that the expression "science knows" (*i.e.,* "knowledge knows") is pure tautology. But our rhetoric seems to get around this by implying that science is *the* knowledge. Other knowledges may contain elements of quackery, and may reflect the selfish aims of the knower; but "science," once we have given the word its incorporation, is the undiluted essence of knowledge. The word as it comes to us then is a little pathetic in its appeal, inasmuch as it reflects the deeply human feeling that somewhere somehow there must be people who know things "as they are." Once God or his ministry was the depository of such knowledge, but now, with the general decay of religious faith, it is the scientists who must speak *ex cathedra,* whether they wish to or not.

The term "modern" shares in the rhetorical forces of the others thus far discussed, and stands not far below the top.

Its place in the general ordering is intelligible through the same history. Where progress is real, there is a natural presumption that the latest will be the best. Hence it is generally thought that to describe anything as "modern" is to credit it with all the improvements which have been made up to now. Then by a transference the term is applied to realms where valuation is, or ought to be, of a different source. In consequence, we have "modern living" urged upon us as an ideal; "the modern mind" is mentioned as something superior to previous minds; sometimes the modifier stands alone as an epithet of approval: "to become modern" or "to sound modern" are expressions that carry valuation. It is of course idle not to expect an age to feel that some of its ways and habits of mind are the best; but the extensive transformations of the past hundred years seem to have given "modern" a much more decisive meaning. It is as if a difference of degree had changed into a différence of kind. But the very fact that a word is not used very analytically may increase its rhetorical potency, as we shall see later in connection with a special group of terms.

Another word definitely high up in the hierarchy we have outlined is "efficient." It seems to have acquired its force through a kind of no-nonsense connotation. If a thing is efficient, it is a good adaptation of means to ends, with small loss through friction. Thus as a word expressing a good understanding and management of cause and effect, it may have a fairly definite referent; but when it is lifted above this and made to serve as a term of general endorsement, we have to be on our guard against the stratagems of evil rhetoric. When we find, to cite a familiar example, the phrase "efficiency apartments" used to give an attractive aspect to inadequate dwellings, we may suspect the motive behind such juxtaposition. In many similar cases, "efficient," which is a term above reproach in engineering and physics, is made to hold our attention where ethical and aesthetic considerations are entitled to priority. Certain notorious forms of government and certain brutal forms of warfare are undeniably efficient; but here the featuring of efficiency unfairly narrows the question.

Another term which might seem to have a different provenance but which participates in the impulse we have been studying is "American." One must first recognize the element of national egotism which makes this a word of approval with us, but there are reasons for saying that the force of "American" is much more broadly based than this. "This is the American way" or "It is the American thing to do" are expressions whose intent will not seem at all curious to the average American. Now the peculiar effect that is intended here comes from the circumstance that "American" and "progressive" have an area of synonymity. The Western World has long stood as a symbol for the future; and accordingly there has been a very wide tendency in this country, and also I believe among many people in Europe, to identify that which is American with that which is destined to be. And this is much the same as identifying it with the achievements of "progress." The typical American is quite fatuous in this regard: to him America is the goal toward which all creation moves; and he judges a country's civilization by its resemblance to the American model. The matter of changing nationalities brings out this point very well. For a citizen of a European country to become a citizen of the United States is considered natural and right, and I have known those so transferring their nationality to be congratulated upon their good sense and their anticipated good fortune. On the contrary, when an American takes out British citizenship (French or German would be worse), this transference is felt to be a little scandalous. It is regarded as somehow perverse, or as going against the stream of things. Even some of our intellectuals grow uneasy over the action of Henry James and T. S. Eliot, and the masses cannot comprehend it at all. Their adoption of British citizenship is not mere defection from a country; it is treason to history. If Americans wish to become Europeans, what has happened to the hope of the world? is, I imagine, the question at the back of their minds. The tremendous spread of American fashions in behavior and entertainment must add something to the impetus, but I believe the original source to be this prior idea that America, typifying "progress," is what the remainder of the world is trying to be like.

It follows naturally that in the popular consciousness of this country, "un-American" is the ultimate in negation. An anecdote will serve to illustrate this. Several years ago a leading cigarette manufacturer in this country had reason to believe that very damaging reports were being circulated about his product. The reports were such that had they not been stopped, the sale of this brand of cigarettes might have been reduced. The company thereupon inaugurated an extensive advertising campaign, the object of which was to halt these rumors in the most effective way possible. The concocters of the advertising copy evidently concluded after due deliberation that the strongest term of condemnation which could be conceived was "un-American," for this was the term employed in the campaign. Soon the newspapers were filled with advertising rebuking this "un-American" type of depreciation which had injured their sales. From examples such as this we may infer that "American" stands not only for what is forward in history, but also for what is ethically superior, or at least for a standard of fairness not matched by other nations.

And as long as the popular mind carries this impression, it will be futile to protest against such titles as "The Committee on un-American activities." While "American" and "un-American" continue to stand for these polar distinctions, the average citizen is not going to find much wrong with a group set up to investigate what is "un-American" and therefore reprehensible. At the same time, however, it would strike him as most droll if the British were to set up a "Committee on un-British Activities" or the French a "Committee on un-French Activities." The American, like other nationals, is not apt to be much better than he has been taught, and he has been taught systematically that his country is a special creation. That is why some of his ultimate terms seem to the general view provincial, and why he may be moved to polarities which represent only local poles.

If we look within the area covered by "American," however, we find significant changes in the position of terms which are reflections of cultural and ideological changes. Among the once powerful but now waning terms are those expressive of the pioneer ideal of ruggedness and self-sufficiency. In the space of fifty years or less we have seen the phrase "two-fisted American" pass from the category of highly effective images to that of comic anachronisms. Generally, whoever talks the older language of strenuosity is regarded as a reactionary, it being assumed by social democrats that a socially organized world is one in which cooperation removes the necessity for struggle. Even the rhetorical trump cards of the 1920's, which Sinclair Lewis treated with such satire, are comparatively impotent today, as the new social consciousness causes terms of centrally planned living to move toward the head of the series.

Other terms not necessarily connected with the American story have passed a zenith of influence and are in decline; of these perhaps the once effective "history" is the most interesting example. It is still to be met in such expressions as "History proves" and "History teaches"; yet one feels that it has lost the force it possessed in the previous century. Then it was easy for Byron—"the orator in poetry"—to write, "History with all her volumes vast has but one page"; or for the commemorative speaker to deduce profound lessons from history. But people today seem not to find history so eloquent. A likely explanation is that history, taken as whole, is conceptual rather than factual, and therefore a skepticism has developed as to what it teaches. Moreover, since the teachings of history are principally moral, ethical, or religious, they must encounter today that threshold resentment of anything which savors of the prescriptive. Since "history" is inseparable from judgment of historical fact, there has to be a considerable community of mind before history can be allowed to have a voice. Did the overthrow of Napoleon represent "progress" in history or the reverse? I should say that the most common rhetorical uses of "history" at the present are by intellectuals, whose personal philosophy can provide it with some kind of definition, and by journalists, who seem to use it unreflectively. For the contemporary masses it is substantially true that "history is bunk."

An instructive example of how a coveted term can be monopolized may be seen in "allies." Three times within the memory of those still young, "allies" (often capitalized) has been used to distinguish those fighting on our side from the enemy. During the First World War it was a supreme term; during the Second World War it was again used with effect; and at the time of the present writing it is being used to designate that nondescript combination fighting in the name of the United Nations in Korea. The curious fact about the use of this term is that in each case the enemy also has been constituted of "allies." In the First World War Germany, Austria-Hungary, and Turkey were "allies"; in the Second, Germany and Italy; and in the present conflict the North Koreans and the Chinese and perhaps the Russians are "allies." But in the rhetorical situation it is not possible to refer to them as "allies," since we reserve that term for the alliance representing our side. The reason for such restriction is that when men or nations are "allied," it is implied that they are united on some sound principle or for some good cause. Lying at the source of this feeling is the principle discussed by Plato, that friendship can exist only among the good, since good is an integrating force and evil a disintegrating one. We do not, for example, refer to a band of thieves as "the allies" because that term would impute laudable motives. By confining the term to our side we make an evaluation in our favor. We thus style ourselves the group joined for purposes of good. If we should allow it to be felt for a moment that the opposed combination is also made up of allies, we should concede that they are united by a principle, which in war is never done. So as the usage goes, we are always allies in war and the enemy is just the enemy, regardless of how many nations he has been able to confederate. Here is clearly another instance of how tendencies may exist in even the most innocent-seeming language.

Now let us turn to the terms of repulsion. Some terms of repulsion are also ultimate in the sense of standing at the end of the series, and no survey of the vocabulary can ignore these prime repellants. The counterpart of the "god term" is the "devil term," and it has already been suggested that with us "un-American" comes nearest to filling that role. Sometimes, however, currents of politics and popular feeling cause something more specific to be placed in that position. There seems indeed to be some obscure psychic law which compels every nation to have in its national imagination an enemy. Perhaps this is but a version of the tribal need for a scapegoat, or for something which will personify "the adversary." If a nation did not have an enemy, an enemy would have to be invented to take care of those expressions of scorn and hatred to which peoples must give vent. When another political state is not available to receive the discharge of such emotions, then a class will be chosen, or a race, or a type, or a political faction, and this will be held up to a practically standardized form of repudiation. Perhaps the truth is that we need the enemy in order to define ourselves, but I will not here venture further into psychological complexities. In this type of study it will be enough to recall that during the first half century of our nation's existence, "Tory" was such a devil term. In the period following our Civil War, "rebel" took its place in the Northern section and "Yankee" in the Southern, although in the previous epoch both of these had been terms of esteem. Most readers will remember that during the First World War "pro-German" was a term of destructive force. During the Second World War "Nazi" and "Fascist" carried about equal power to condemn, and then, following the breach with Russia, "Communist" displaced them both. Now "Communist" is beyond any rival the devil term, and as such it is employed even by the American president when he feels the need of a strong rhetorical point.

A singular truth about these terms is that, unlike several which were examined in our favorable list, they defy any real analysis. That is to say, one cannot explain how they generate their peculiar force of repudiation. One only recognizes them as publicly-agreed-upon devil terms. It is the same with all. "Tory" persists in use, though it has long lost any connection with redcoats and British domination. Analysis of "rebel" and "Yankee" only turns up embarrassing contradictions of position. Similarly we have all seen "Nazi" and "Fascist" used without rational perception; and we see this now, in even greater degree, with "Communist." However one might like to reject such usage as mere ignorance, to do so would only evade a very important problem. Most likely these are instances of the "charismatic term," which will be discussed in detail presently.

No student of contemporary usage can be unmindful of the curious reprobative force which has been acquired by the term "prejudice." Etymologically it signifies nothing more than a prejudgment, or a judgment before all the facts are in; and since all of us have to proceed to a great extent on judgments of that kind, the word should not be any more exciting than "hypothesis." But in its rhetorical applications "prejudice" presumes far beyond that. It is used, as a matter of fact, to characterize unfavorably any value judgment whatever. If "blue" is said to be a better color than "red," that is prejudice. If people of outstanding cultural achievement are praised through contrast with another people, that is prejudice. If one mode of life is presented as superior to another, that is prejudice. And behind all is the implication, if not the declaration, that it is un-American to be prejudiced.

I suspect that what the users of this term are attempting, whether consciously or not, is to sneak "prejudiced" forward as an uncontested term, and in this way to disarm the opposition by making all positional judgments reprehensible. It must be observed in passing that no people are so prejudiced in the sense of being committed to valuations as those who are engaged in castigating others for prejudice. What they expect is that they can nullify the prejudices of those who oppose them, and then get their own installed in the guise of the *sensus communis*. Mark Twain's statement, "I know that I am prejudiced in this matter, but I would be ashamed of myself if I weren't" is a therapeutic insight into the process; but it will take more than a witticism to make headway against the repulsive force gathered behind "prejudice."

If the rhetorical use of the term has any rational content, this probably comes through a chain of deductions from the nature of democracy; and we know that in controversies centered about the meaning of democracy, the air is usually filled with cries of "prejudice." If democracy is taken crudely to mean equality, as it very frequently is, it is then a contradiction of democracy to assign inferiority and superiority on whatever grounds. But since the whole process of evaluation is a process of such assignment, the various inequalities which are left when it has done its work are contradictions of this root notion and hence are "prejudice"—the assumption of course being that when all the facts are in, these inequalities will be found illusory. The man who dislikes a certain class or race or style has merely not taken pains to learn that it is just as good as any other. If all inequality is deception, then superiorities must be accounted the products of immature judgment. This affords plausible ground, as we have suggested, for the coupling of "prejudice" and "ignorance."

Before leaving the subject of the ordered series of good and bad terms, one feels obliged to say something about the way in which hierarchies can be inverted. Under the impulse of strong frustration there is a natural tendency to institute a pretense that the best is the worst and the worst is the best—an inversion sometimes encountered in literature and in social deportment. The best illustration for purpose of study here comes from a department of speech which I shall call "GI rhetoric." The average American youth, put into uniform, translated to a new and usually barren environment, and imbued from many sources with a mission of killing, has undergone a pretty severe dislocation. All of this runs counter to the benevolent platitudes on which he was brought up, and there is little ground for wonder if he adopts the inverted pose. This is made doubly likely by the facts that he is at a passionate age and that he is thrust into an atmosphere of superinduced excitement. It would be unnatural for him not to acquire a rhetoric of strong impulse and of contumacious tendency.

What he does is to make an almost complete inversion. In this special world of his he recoils from those terms used by politicians and other civilians and by the "top brass" when they are enunciating public sentiments. Dropping the conventional terms of attraction, this uprooted and specially focussed young man puts in their place terms of repulsion. To be more specific, where the others use terms reflecting love, hope, and charity, he uses almost exclusively terms connected with the excretory and reproductive functions. Such terms comprise what Kenneth Burke has ingeniously called "the imagery of killing." By an apparently universal psychological law, faeces and the act of defecation are linked with the idea of killing, of destruction, of total repudiation—perhaps the word "elimination" would comprise the whole body of notions. The reproductive act is associated especially with the idea of aggressive exploitation. Consequently when the GI feels that he must give his speech a proper show of spirit, he places the symbols for these things in places which would normally be filled by prestige terms from the "regular" list. For specimens of such language presented in literature, the reader is referred to the fiction of Ernest Hemingway and Norman Mailer.

Anyone who has been compelled to listen to such rhetoric will recall the monotony of the vocabulary and the vehemence of the delivery. From these two characteristics we may infer a great need and a narrow means of satisfaction, together with the tension which must result from maintaining so arduous an inversion. Whereas previously the aim had been to love (in the broad sense) it is now to kill; whereas it had been freedom and individuality, it is now restriction and brutalization. In taking revenge for a change which so contradicts his upbringing he is quite capable, as the evidence has already proved, of defiantly placing the lower level above the higher. Sometimes a clever GI will invent combinations and will effect metaphorical departures, but the ordinary ones are limited to a reiteration of the stock terms—to a reiteration, with emphasis of intonation, upon "the imagery of killing."[2] Taken as a whole, this rhetoric is a clear if limited example of how the machine may be put in reverse—of how, consequently, a sort of devil worship may get into language.

A similar inversion of hierarchy is to be seen in the world

[2] Compare Sherwood Anderson's analysis of the same phenomenon in A Story Teller's Story (New York, 1928), 198: "There was in the factories where I worked and where the efficient Ford type of man was just beginning his dull reign this strange and futile outpouring of men's lives in vileness through their lips. Ennui was at work. The talk of the men about me was not Rabelaisian. In old Rabelais there was the salt of infinite wit and I have no doubt that the Rabelasian flashes that came from our own Lincoln, Washington, and others had point and a flare to them. But in the factories and in army camps!"

of competitive sports, although to a lesser extent. The great majority of us in the Western World have been brought up under the influence, direct or indirect, of Christianity, which is a religion of extreme altruism. Its terms of value all derive from a law of self-effacement and of consideration for others, and these terms tend to appear whenever we try to rationalize or vindicate our conduct. But in the world of competitive sports, the direction is opposite: there one is applauded for egotistic display and for success at the expense of others—should one mention in particular American professional baseball? Thus the terms with which an athlete is commended will generally point away from the direction of Christian passivity, although when an athlete's character is described for the benefit of the general public, some way is usually found to place him in the other ethos, as by calling attention to his natural kindness, his interest in children, or his readiness to share his money.

Certainly many of the contradictions of our conduct may be explained through the presence of these small inverted hierarchies. When, to cite one further familiar example, the acquisitive, hard-driving local capitalist is made the chief lay official of a Christian church, one knows that in a definite area there has been a transvaluation of values.

Earlier in the chapter we referred to terms of considerable potency whose referents it is virtually impossible to discover or to construct through imagination. I shall approach this group by calling them "charismatic terms." It is the nature of the charismatic term to have a power which is not derived, but which is in some mysterious way given. By this I mean to say that we cannot explain their compulsiveness through referents of objectively known character and tendency. We normally "understand" a rhetorical term's appeal through its connection with something we apprehend, even when we object morally to the source of the impulse. Now "progress" is an understandable term in this sense, since it rests upon certain observable if not always commendable aspects of our world. Likewise the referential support of "fact" needs no demonstrating. These derive their force from a reading of palpable circumstance. But in charismatic terms we are confronted with a different creation: these terms seem to have broken loose somehow and to operate independently of referential connections (although in some instances an earlier history of referential connection may be made out). Their meaning seems inexplicable unless we accept the hypothesis that their content proceeds out of a popular will that they *shall* mean something. In effect, they are rhetorical by common consent, or by "charisma." As is the case with charismatic authority, where the populace gives the leader a power which can by no means be explained through his personal attributes, and permits him to use it effectively and even arrogantly, the charismatic term is given its load of impulsion without reference, and it functions by convention. The number of such terms is small in any one period, but they are perhaps the most efficacious terms of all.

Such rhetorical sensibility as I have leads me to believe that one of the principal charismatic terms of our age is "freedom." The greatest sacrifices that contemporary man is called upon to make are demanded in the name of "freedom"; yet the referent which the average man attaches to this word is most obscure. Burke's dictum that "freedom inheres in something sensible" has not prevented its breaking loose from all anchorages. And the evident truth that the average man, given a choice between exemption from responsibility and responsibility, will choose the latter, makes no impression against its power. The fact, moreover, that the most extensive use of the term is made by modern politicians and statesmen in an effort to get men to assume more responsibility (in the form of military service, increased taxes, abridgement of rights, etc.) seems to carry no weight either.[3] The fact that what the American pioneer considered freedom has become wholly impossible to the modern apartment-dwelling metropolitan seems not to have damaged its potency. Unless we accept some philosophical interpretation, such as the proposition that freedom consists only in the discharge of responsibility, there seems no possibility of a correlation between the use of the word and circumstantial reality. Yet "freedom" remains an ultimate term, for which people are asked to yield up their first-born.

There is plenty of evidence that "democracy" is becoming the same kind of term. The variety of things it is used to symbolize is too weird and too contradictory for one to find even a core meaning in present-day usages. More important than this for us is the fact, noted by George Orwell, that people resist any attempt to define democracy, as if to connect it with a clear and fixed referent were to vitiate it. It may well be that such resistance to definition of democracy arises from a subconscious fear that a term defined in the usual manner has its charisma taken away. The situation then is that "democracy" means "be democratic," and that means exhibit a certain attitude which you can learn by imitating your fellows.

If rationality is measured by correlations and by analyzable content, then these terms are irrational; and there is one further modern development in the creation of such terms which is strongly suggestive of irrational impulse. This is

[3] One is inevitably reminded of the slogan of Oceania in Orwell's *Nineteen Eighty-four:* "Freedom is Slavery."

the increasing tendency to employ in the place of the term itself an abbreviated or telescoped form—which form is nearly always used with even more reckless assumption of authority. I seldom read the abbreviation "U S" in the newspapers without wincing at the complete arrogance of its rhetorical tone. Daily we see "US Cracks Down on Communists"; "U S Gives OK to Atomic Weapons"; "U S Shocked by Death of Official." Who or what is this "U S"? It is clear that "U S" does not suggest a union of forty-eight states having republican forms of government and held together by a constitution of expressly delimited authority. It suggests rather an abstract force out of a new world of forces, whose will is law and whom the individual citizen has no way to placate. Consider the individual citizen confronted by "U S" or "FBI." As long as terms stand for identifiable organs of government, the citizen feels that he knows the world he moves around in, but when the forces of government are referred to by these bloodless abstractions, he cannot avoid feeling that they are one thing and he another. Let us note while dealing with this subject the enormous proliferation of such forms during the past twenty years or so. If "U S" is the most powerful and prepossessing of the group, it drags behind it in train the previously mentioned "FBI," and "NPA," "ERP," "FDIC," "WPA," "HOLC," and "OSS," to take a few at random. It is a fact of ominous significance that this use of foreshortened forms is preferred by totalitarians, both the professed and the disguised. Americans were hearing the terms "OGPU," "AMTORG," and "NEP" before their own government turned to large-scale state planning. Since then we have spawned them ourselves, and, it is to be feared, out of similar impulse. George Orwell, one of the truest humanists of our age, has described the phenomenon thus: "Even in the early decades of the twentieth century, telescoped words and phrases had been one of the characteristic features of political language; and it had been noticed that the tendency to use abbreviations of this kind was most marked in totalitarian countries and totalitarian organizations. Examples were such words as Nazi, Gestapo, Comintern, Inprecor, Agitprop."[4]

I venture to suggest that what this whole trend indicates is an attempt by the government, as distinguished from the people, to confer charismatic authority. In the earlier specimens of charismatic terms we were examining, we beheld something like the creation of a spontaneous general will. But these later ones of truncated form are handed down from above, and their potency is by fiat of whatever group is administering in the name of democracy. Actually the process is no more anomalous than the issuing of pamphlets to soldiers telling them whom they shall hate and whom they shall like (or try to like), but the whole business of switching impulse on and off from a central headquarters has very much the meaning of *Gleichschaltung* as that word has been interpreted for me by a native German. Yet it is a disturbing fact that such process should increase in times of peace, because the persistent use of such abbreviations can only mean a serious divorce between rhetorical impulse and rational thought. When the ultimate terms become a series of bare abstractions, the understanding of power is supplanted by a worship of power, and in our condition this can mean only state worship.

It is easy to see, however, that a group determined upon control will have as one of its first objectives the appropriation of sources of charismatic authority. Probably the surest

[4] "Principles of Newspeak," *Nineteen Eighty-four* (New York, 1949), 310.

way to detect the fabricated charismatic term is to identify those terms ordinarily of limited power which are being moved up to the front line. That is to say, we may suspect the act of fabrication when terms of secondary or even tertiary rhetorical rank are pushed forward by unnatural pressure into ultimate positions. This process can nearly always be observed in times of crisis. During the last war, for example, "defense" and "war effort" were certainly regarded as culminative terms. We may say this because almost no one thinks of these terms as the natural sanctions of his mode of life. He may think thus of "progress" or "happiness" or even "freedom"; but "defense" and "war effort" are ultimate sanctions only when measured against an emergency situation. When the United States was preparing for entry into that conflict, every departure from our normal way of life could be justified as a "defense" measure. Plants making bombs to be dropped on other continents were called "defense" plants. Correspondingly, once the conflict had been entered, everything that was done in military or civilian areas was judged by its contribution to the "war effort." This last became for a period of years the supreme term: not God or Heaven or happiness, but successful effort in the war. It was a term to end all other terms or a rhetoric to silence all other rhetoric. No one was able to make his claim heard against "the war effort."

It is most important to realize, therefore, that under the stress of feeling or preoccupation, quite secondary terms can be moved up to the position of ultimate terms, where they will remain until reflection is allowed to resume sway. There are many signs to show that the term "aggressor" is now undergoing such manipulation. Despite the fact that almost no term is more difficult to correlate with objective phenomena, it is being rapidly promoted to ultimate "bad" term. The likelihood is that "agressor" will soon become a depository for all the resentments and fears which naturally arise in a people. As such, it will function as did "infidel" in the mediaeval period and as "reactionary" has functioned in the recent past. Manifestly it is of great advantage to a nation bent upon organizing its power to be able to stigmatize some neighbor as "aggressor," so that the term's capacity for irrational assumption is a great temptation for those who are not moral in their use of rhetoric. This passage from natural or popular to state-engendered charisma produces one of the most dangerous lesions of modern society.

An ethics of rhetoric requires that ultimate terms be ultimate in some rational sense. The only way to achieve that objective is through an ordering of our own minds and our own passions. Every one of psychological sophistication knows that there is a pleasure in willed perversity, and the setting up of perverse shibboleths is a fairly common source of that pleasure. War cries, school slogans, coterie passwords, and all similar expressions are examples of such creation. There may be areas of play in which these are nothing more than a diversion; but there are other areas in which such expressions lure us down the roads of hatred and tragedy. That is the tendency of all words of false or "engineered" charisma. They often sound like the very gospel of one's society, but in fact they betray us; they get us to do what the adversary of the human being wants us to do. It is worth considering whether the real civil disobedience must not begin with our language.

Lastly, the student of rhetoric must realize that in the contemporary world he is confronted not only by evil practitioners, but also, and probably to an unprecedented degree, by men who are conditioned by the evil created by others. The machinery of propagation and inculcation is today so immense that no one avoids entirely the assimilation and use of some terms which have a downward tendency. It is especially easy to pick up a tone without realizing its trend. Perhaps the best that any of us can do is to hold a dialectic with himself to see what the wider circumferences of his terms of persuasion are. This process will not only improve the consistency of one's thinking but it will also, if the foregoing analysis is sound, prevent his becoming a creature of evil public forces and a victim of his own thoughtless rhetoric.

Relativism and the Use of Language will be pre-sented [at Sea Island, Georgia] during the pres-ent month. There is a good bit still to do . . . ; I think some of my distinctions are not clear enough. . . . But it was the best I could do after three months of wrestling with what seemed the hardest subject I ever tackled in this field.

—RICHARD M. WEAVER TO RALPH T. EUBANKS
September 2, 1959

The question raised in this essay lies at the very heart of Weaver's view of the function of language. The issue—hardest he ever tackled—is this: "What is the relationship between words and the extramental order they symbolize?"

To Weaver it was clear that language could not remain "pure"; he knew that words must change and that mean-ings "do shift over a period of time." And yet he was equally certain that "meaning cannot be judged as relative simply to time and place."

The analysis of "Relativism and the Use of Language" proceeds upon the assumption that "language is a humanis-tic creation" in which "meaning and value are closely bound." From this underlying assumption emerges the idea of the "linguistic covenant" and the belief that "both effec-tive and right ways of saying things can be taught."

Relativism
and the Use of Language

Nor do I think it a matter of little moment
whether the language of a people be vitiated or
refined, whether the popular idiom be erroneous
or correct. . . . It is the opinion of Plato, that
changes in the dress and habits of the citizens
portend great changes and commotions in the
state; and I am inclined to believe that when the
language in common use in any country becomes
irregular and depraved, it is followed by their
ruin or their degradation. For what do terms
used without skill or meaning, which are at once
corrupt and misapplied, denote but a people list-
less, supine, and ripe for servitude? On the contrary, we have never heard of any people or state
which has not flourished in some degree of pros-
perity as long as their language has retained its
elegance and its purity.

—MILTON TO BENEDETTO BONOMATTHAI,
September 10, 1638[1]

[1] *The Prose Works of John Milton* (London, 1806), I, xi–xii.

THE EPIGRAPH from Milton is included here to represent a rather general feeling that a society cannot remain
harmonious and healthy unless its use of language remains
pure. "Pure" in this sense means stable, because fixed with
respect to semantic references. More precisely, the feeling is
that people cannot express the same idea or take the same
attitude toward the same thing or agree on a policy which
all will follow alike unless there is a certain minimal identity in the signification of the signs they employ, and the
most common of these signs are linguistic. Confusion and
conflict may result when the people engaged in any enter-
prise, which would include, of course, the maintaining of a
state, find that their words are no longer reliable communi-
cators of ideas and feelings. In such cases, where words
have ceased to be a fixed medium of exchange, each party
that feels misunderstood because its meaning was not received in the form intended may react with passion, and
this can be the beginning of internecine strife. It will be
recalled that the United States Senate debated for thirty
years whether the term "constitution" could be translated
"compact." This difference was eventually settled by a
bloody civil war. In our own time we have had ample
occasion to notice how words of critical importance are
used in varying and even conflicting senses. For the people
of most Western countries, "democracy" means "government by the people"; for those in the communist world, it
means "government of the people" by an elite presumed to
be wiser than they are. "Liberalism" has been so twisted
and perverted that it may be beyond any hope of rehabilitation in our time. Even a term like "peace," whose referent
used to be a certain idea of order, now seems hard to match
consistently with any idea. "Peace" and "war" have become

hard to disentangle, and there seems to be a rather wide-spread mentality today that understands "peace" as the successful imposition of one's will upon resisters.

In opposition to this is another view, generated by the popularity of modern relativism, which is that semantic reference must be a relative affair. It is not easy to state this in the form of a precise theory, but the general sense seems to be that language, like every other phenomenon, has to be viewed as part of a changing world. There are, accordingly, no fixed significations. The meaning that a word has will depend upon the time and place in which it is used and the point of view of the user. Meaning is thus contingent and evolving. There is no absolute position from which the application of a word can be judged "right" or "wrong." There can be only shrewd estimates as to what the majority of men will accept. As the world changes, meaning changes too, and we can only hope that the two will proceed *pari passu*. The relativist is, of course, pleased rather than otherwise that language offers no exception to, or way of escape from, his world of relativity.

An awareness of the problems growing out of man's dependence upon words for communication is at least as old as the Greeks. It led Plato, in the *Cratylus*, to ask, with the typically Greek direct approach, whether there is not a natural rightness to the names of things. Does every object that bears a name have a kind of proprietary right to that name because of a definite (and possibly iconic) relationship between the two? Cratylus appears in the dialogue as the upholder of a doctrine that "everything has a right name of its own, which comes by nature, and . . . a name is not just whatever people call a thing by agreement, just as a piece of their own voice applied to a thing, but . . .

there is a kind of inherent correctness in names, which is the same for all men, both Greeks and barbarians."[2] After a long discussion in which Socrates puts this theory to a number of tests, the idea that names have an essential rightness because they are imitations of the realities named is given up as inadequate, and the necessity of some element of convention is admitted. I believe that no serious student of language today, with the exception of a few advocates of "semantics" who are not very well grounded in language study, argues as a general thesis that there is some aboriginal iconic connection between a word and what the word stands for. (A few indisputable examples of onomatopoeia may have to be excepted.) Plato could not prove it for the Greek language, in spite of many ingenious attempts in this dialogue, and the immensely greater knowledge of linguistic variety that we have today seems to remove the problem from consideration.

The obscurity of the whole matter of semantic relationship, however, continues to create illusions. Some of these are due to the work of popular writers offering easy solutions, most of whom seem to take vaguely relativist positions. The sum of their doctrine appears to be that if we will simply adjust our vocabulary to changing external reality, most of the world's ignorance and prejudice will be removed. This might do no more harm than other nostrums, except that it finds reception among people whose use of language has a very practical bearing upon society. For in addition to permeating the public mind to an appreciable extent, it seems to have influenced some of our jurists, whose very prerogative makes them "definers," and whose definitions are, of course, binding in a legal sense.

[2] *Cratylus,* 383b.

Here are two examples. Mr. Justice Holmes is on record as saying, "A word is not a crystal, transparent and unchanged; it is the skin of a living thought and may vary greatly in color and content according to the circumstances and time in which it is used."[3] Chief Justice Vinson observed: "Nothing is more certain in modern society than the principle that all concepts are relative: a name, a phrase, a standard, has meaning only when associated with the considerations which gave birth to the nomenclature."[4] The first of these pronouncements stresses the relationship between a word and the circumstances under which it is used. The second states outright that all names and phrases are relative to the situations that gave birth to them and introduces a further difficulty by maintaining that this principle has special application to modern society. I would not deny that some element of truth could be extracted from both observations, yet it would have to be hedged about very cautiously. Taken as a philosophy of language without careful interpretation, such statements are insufficient and misleading. In these instances, the source causes them to pass readily into popular thinking.

The difficulty of the whole problem makes us wonder whether some help cannot be found by investigating the ultimate origin of language. Yet this turns out to be a subject of the utmost perplexity. None of the theories of language thus far propounded impresses us as convincing, and some of them appear almost childishly naive. Attempts have been made to show that man first learned to speak by imitating the sounds of nature. Other attempts have been

---

[3] Quoted in Clinton Rossiter, *Conservatism in America* (New York, 1955), 4.
[4] In his opinion upholding the conviction of eleven Communist leaders. See New York *Times*, June 5, 1951.

made to trace language to instinctive cries. Still other attempts have been made to show that the roots of words found in cognate languages express certain temporal and spatial relations. But why these root forms were chosen for these particular perceptions, why they are not found in all languages as well as the Indo-Germanic, and how they were elaborated upon to produce words capable of complex signification are questions that go unanswered.[5]

About all that can be affirmed with confidence is that language is a very ancient creation of man. Edward Sapir is of the opinion that it "antedated even the lowliest developments of material culture, [and] that these developments, in fact, were not strictly possible until language, the tool of significant expression, had itself taken shape."[6] He furthermore believes that not even interjections are merely instinctive; he thinks that they express some feeling about the occasion molded or transformed by a mentality that is qualitatively human.[7]

It therefore seems impossible to arrive at any theory of the "rightness" of the meaning of words by studying their first origin and by tracing their early evolutionary development. The origin remains wrapped in mystery, and there are those who will say that language is a divine gift to man, like his soul. The best resource left to us is to look at its constitution and function to see what light these shed upon semantic change and upon the social and cultural problems connected with this.

Language, as I conceive it, is a social and cultural crea-

[5] For a survey of theories regarding the origin of language, see Mario Pei, *The Story of Language* (Philadelphia, 1949), 18–20.
[6] Edward Sapir, *Language* (New York, 1921), 23.
[7] *Ibid.,* 4.

tion functioning somehow within the psychic constitution
of those who use it. The scope of the reference of words is
accordingly determined by forces within the psychic constitution and not outside it. The question of stability in
language cannot be considered apart from the psychic stability of the cultural group. And by the same inference the
reason for changes in language, whether of the kind we
approve or disapprove, will have to be sought in that prime
source. All this may seem to border on a mystical account
of what, after all, is an empirical fact, subject in several of
its aspects to direct observation. Yet the problem of meaning remains elusive after observations of this kind have
been made.

I am inclined to agree with W. M. Urban, in his *Language and Reality*, that the situation is the reverse of what
is usually conceived.[8] It is not that things give meaning to
words; it is that meaning makes things "things." It does not
make things in their subsistence; but it does make things in
their discreteness for the understanding. Extramental reality may itself be a nameless flow of causality, but when we
apperceive it, we separate it into "discretes" such as
"house," "tree," "mountain." And naming follows hard
upon this, if, indeed, it is not an essential part of the
process itself. Communication and cognition thus seem
very closely related. To know a thing is not to arrive finally
at some direct perception of a property, as Locke suggests,
but to form some ideal construct of it, in which meaning
and value are closely bound. Theories of meaning that
include only the symbol and the thing symbolized leave out
of account the interpreter. But there can be no such thing

[8] W. M. Urban, *Language and Reality* (New York, 1939), 105–106.

as meaning, in the sense of understanding, unless there is a third entity, the human being, who brings the two together in a system of comprehension.

The central point of this essay is that language cannot be viewed as a merely naturalistic phenomenon, subject only to forces that have their source in the objective world and, therefore, varying simply according to time and place.

As a starting point for the analysis of language, a statement which Shelley makes, in his "A Defence of Poetry," seems better than anything I have found in the writings of the scientific linguists. In the course of a passage dealing with the relationship of language and poetry, he says: "Language is arbitrarily produced by the imagination and has relation to thoughts alone."[9] This is equivalent to affirming that language is a humanistic creation, whose function cannot be understood except with reference to the realm of the mind. I shall qualify this later on, but taken as it is, it leaves us in position to deal with one of the paradoxes about language, which is (1) that there is no "natural" relationship between a word and the thing it stands for, and (2) that, nevertheless, the meanings of words cannot be changed by an individual on his own motion. An effective change cannot be made unless it is endorsed by that part of humanity to which one belongs linguistically. But since change is a fact of language, this leaves the question of who the real arbiters of a change are when it is made. I would answer that they are those who share most fully in what Shelley referred to as the imagination. I would here borrow an analogy that Croce uses in speaking of art when he says that all men are artists, but that some are great and some are small ones. In the same way, all men

[9] Percy Bysshe Shelley, *Prose Works* (London, 1888), II, 6.

are "imaginers," but some men are small ones and some are great. Those who have the greatest insight into what words should mean are those with the greatest imaginative power.

Imagination in the sense used here is an absolute faculty. Not in actual cases, but ideally, it is commensurate with humanity itself. It is capable of telling us theoretically exactly what every word must mean because it is the imagination that holds in contemplation all the various meanings that have to remain discrete and yet have somehow to function together in coherent discourse. Just as those who have the best judgment in art approximate absolute taste, so those who have the best judgment in words approximate absolute imagination. All of us have had the experience of finding a particularly felicitous phrase in poetry and of feeling: "This is what the word really means; he has hit it closer than anyone has ever hit it before." I assume that we could not have this feeling unless two things were present: (1) our everyday, more or less obtuse understanding of the word, and (2) an awareness that there is a meaning beyond this, which our own imagination had not permitted us to attain. It is the man of greater imagination who helps to raise our imagination toward the absolute correctness of meaning.

The problem of deciding upon the correct meaning of words, then, is not one of external measurement, but one of internal receptivity or capability. If we share to a large extent in that mutuality of spirit which makes meaning possible, we are receptive to true meanings; if we do not, we may accept wrong or perverted ones. And since there is no way of getting outside the human imagination to decide otherwise what a word should mean, we are compelled to realize that the most imaginative users of language are those who are going to have the greatest influence upon vocabulary in the long run. We realize further that the ones who name things in this way have a great influence in determining how the things will be regarded by our customs and laws. This is why Shelley, in that famous concluding sentence of "A Defence of Poetry," could call poets "the unacknowledged legislators of the world," a claim which might seem a bit of chauvinism in a poet, but which is capable of the most sober kind of defense.

Some such concept of language is required by the undeniable fact of its conventional function. And since words do function conventionally, they must function as deductive instrumentalities. Let us note here that one type of critic today tends to attack language as a means of communication on this very ground—the ground that words are conventional in their meaning and are therefore falsifying. The point of the criticism is that a convention is something abstracted and, therefore, untrue, a generalized sign of the thing itself, which we use because we are unable or unwilling to render the thing in itself in its fullness. A word in this conception is nothing but a stereotype, and "stereotype" is here an expression of disparagement, because it is felt that "typing" anything that is real distorts the thing by presenting it in something less than its full individuality and concreteness. Let us suppose that I make reference to a tree standing in my yard. The term "tree" does not designate the object with any degree of particularity. It does not tell whether the tree is young or old, low or tall, an oak, pine, or maple. The term is, therefore, merely a utility symbol, which I employ in communicating because in my laziness or incompetence I cannot find a fuller and more individualizing way of expressing this tree. If I were really communicating, the argument goes, I would reject the falsifying stereotype and produce something more nearly like the picture of the tree.

But if the analysis I have offered earlier is correct, these critics are beginning at the wrong end. They are assuming that individual real objects are carriers of meaning, that the meaning is found in them as redness is found in an apple, and that it ought to be expressed with the main object of fidelity to the particular. What they overlook is that meaning does not exist in this sense, that it is something that we create for purposes of cognition and communication, and that the ideal construct has the virtue of its ideality.[10]

Hence it appears that they misconceive the function of the word as conventional sign or "typifier." For if it is true that the word conveys something less than the fullness of

[10] The author is aware that in these paragraphs he is going over ground that was well trodden in the Middle Ages. The great controversy over the status of universals, in which Abelard, Aquinas, and William of Ockham were prominent contenders, concerned questions with which the modern student of language and semiotics still has to deal. The position taken in this essay, which perhaps comes closest to that of Abelard, represents an attempt to answer the following question: What is the relationship between words and the extramental order that they symbolize? It is impossible, for reasons we have already seen, to assume a simple correspondence between the two. But, on the other hand, if we say there is no relationship, we abandon the objectivity of knowledge and leave the door open for pure subjectivism or skepticism. This is where Shelley's dictum has to be emended: words do not have relation to thoughts alone; they have relation to the real world *through* thought. The relationship between a word and whatever it stands for is thus an *imputed* relationship, which is the same as saying a relationship in thought. According to Abelard, what is expressed by a general term is in the thing symbolized (and hence the term has objective reference), but it is not in the thing in the form in which it is conceived by the mind. This distinction enables one to affirm that words do have relation to the real order, but that this relation can never be explained by simple analogies based on correspondence, contiguity, or other ideas involving that order. When I say that meaning creates things, I am saying that the mind conceives things in its own way for purposes of communication. It is the logical content of a word that is predicated of a percept, and this brings us back to the fact of language as a closed system, into which the extramental world has no direct mode of ingress. Prior to a more definitive epistemology and metaphysics, it seems impossible to say anything more definitive about the nature of reference.

the thing signified, it is also true that it conveys something more. A word in this role is a generalization. The value of a generalization is that while it leaves out the specific features that are of the individual or of the moment, it expresses features that are general to a class and may be lacking or imperfect in the single instance. What "tree," therefore, expresses is the generic nature of the tree, and so with "house," "city," "man," and all other such terms. In order to make statements that will have applicability over a period of time or in the occurrence of many instances, we have to avail ourselves of these classifiers. Obviously there are many situations in which we wish to say more about a thing than a specific image would convey. To do so, we abstract the common features of many such images, (i.e., we arrive at a general meaning) and use the result as an index to a class of things. I repeat that if something is sacrificed in this process, something is also gained. Those who object to the word because it "stereotypes" are refusing to consider what may be the prime reason for the invention of language. They are forgetting that oftentimes we need to refer to a class of things, to those now out of sight as well as those before our eyes, to those that are past as well as to those that are now existing, and especially to those of the future.

At stake is nothing less than the whole body of general ideas. If we insist upon a point-by-point resemblance of word and particular thing signified, language would have to limp along at a very slow pace. Even ideographs are not really pictures of the things they represent; they are generalized depictions of objects and actions. It must be clear that the very business of a people and the continuity of a cultural tradition depend upon an acceptance of the agreed-upon sign in its extensive application. It is the imagination that sets the bounds of that application and has the privilege of widening and narrowing them.

One of the most interesting criticisms of the conventionalizing property of language, which I desire to notice at length, was made by the late Benjamin Lee Whorf. Whorf became interested in linguistic problems as the result of work he was doing as investigator for a fire insurance company. It was his duty to find out and report the circumstances surrounding the outbreak of fires. In the course of this work he became impressed by the way in which people are misled by what he calls "verbal analogies." He found that accidents sometimes resulted from the fact that people behaved in response to the conventional meanings of words when attention to the actual conditions would have produced a very different kind of behavior. Behavior dictated by the actual circumstances would have prevented an accident.

Here are two incidents he uses to illustrate his point. A group of men were employed around some gasoline drums which they had been told were "empty." Now "empty," just because it conventionally signifies the absence or privation of something, suggests at the same time an incapacity to cause harm (as it would if applied to a gun). But actually "empty" gasoline drums, because they contain vapor, are much more likely to explode than filled ones. Acting on the assumption that these drums were empty and therefore harmless, the men were careless about lighted matches and burning cigarettes and so allowed an explosion to occur. They had been betrayed by the general meaning of "empty" into misinterpreting the actual situation. The second example involves a wood distillation plant, where metal stills were insulated with a composition made from limestone.

No attempt was made to protect the covering from excessive heat or contact of the flame. After a period of use the fire beneath one of the stills spread to the "limestone," which, to everyone's great surprise, burned vigorously. Exposure to acetic acid fumes from the stills had converted part of the limestone (calcium carbonate) to calcium acetate. This, when heated in a fire, decomposes, forming inflammable acetone. Behavior which tolerated fire close to the covering was induced by the use of the name "limestone," which, because it ends in "—stone," implies "incombustibility." [11]

Now these seem to me very interesting, if unfortunate, exceptions to the utility of the generic sense of terms. But my point is that they can be regarded only as exceptions. For every occasion on which the use of a term like "empty" or "stone" leads to misguided action, there must be hundreds or thousands on which it guides the action correctly. In other words, the "class" meaning saves us incomparably more often than it harms us or causes us to have accidents. The analogizing function that these instances are used to deprecate is something we are unable to do without. Numberless necessary actions of our lives are predicated upon assumptions that "empty" does not mean "more dangerous than ever" but less dangerous and that "stone" means "fire-resistant." To the extent that these situations have to be faced as practical problems, I would merely point out that the user of the language had not been as specific as the language easily permits one to be. What was said was true up to a point, but beyond that it was not qualified in the right way. The gasoline drums were empty of liquid, but they were not empty of vapor, and the insulating material was stone in a sense, but it was stone in the

[11] Benjamin Lee Whorf, *Four Articles on Metalinguistics* (Washington: Department of State, 1950), 75–76.

process of chemical transformation. This is a problem that arises at every turn in the use of language. It does not call for denying the predictive "analogizing" function of words, but for making the prediction a little fuller by expressing additional meanings. The meanings that were given needed to be supplemented by other meanings. But these meanings are no more physically attached to the objects than were the other "erroneous" ones. The real task is always to find the right construction for the real order in the logical order.

Believers in the value of language as a convention (and in the connection of this with preserving cultural tradition) are, for such reasons, suspicious of those who take a complacent attitude toward semantic change. They feel that change of meaning is somehow a sign of ignorance or laxity. It represents to them a breaking away from some original standard of "rightness" owing to the user's failure to inform himself fully about the word or to irresponsibility. They wish language to remain pure, and "pure" means in accordance with the old standards of signification. I share the moral impulse that makes them take this stand, but I believe some way will have to be found to take into account more of the realities involved. It seems an irrefragable fact that meanings do shift over a period of time, with a movement hardly more to be resisted than a glacier's. Is there any way of reconciling the ideal of semantic purism with this fact? Is it possible to visualize a kind of gold standard of semantic reference, from which illegitimate departures could be detected? I think it might be possible if we could find some basis for distinguishing between those changes which are "natural" and therefore must be conceded and those which are perverse and should be put down in the interest of intellectual and cultural integrity.

We can begin by noting what some students of language

call "linguistic drift." This is a change, occurring usually over a long span of time, which affects such features as inflection, syntax, and usage. "Drift" suggests some kind of irrational, directionless change, whereas the striking thing about this change is that it seems to manifest direction. It is not an accumulation of random divergences, but a change occurring according to a pattern, which will accept some innovations and reject others. Sapir observes that "linguistic drift has direction. . . . The drift of a language is constituted by the unconscious selection on the part of its speakers of those individual variations that are cumulative in some special direction."[12] In brief, the change is selective and not simply accidental.

Now, there seems to be something corresponding to this that might be denominated "semantic shift." Over a long period of time words will change their references in ways that are not haphazard but are consonant with changes in the general mind. Just what the ultimate cause of the change is seems difficult to ascertain. Perhaps it is the result of an aging of the cultural group that speaks the language, of a sophistication or an assimilation of experience, of the accumulating of past history that inevitably brings with it a change of perspective. Nor do we understand the law of this change. The changes may follow our insights into reality, or they may reflect epiphanies of experience. Usually as the word changes, the meaning keeps polarizing around some idea. The word "dress," in the earliest meaning that can be traced, meant "to make straight." (Hence, "to dress food"; "to dress hides.") It is apparent that something of the core meaning survives in our phrase "to dress oneself." The word "write" traces back to an earlier word

---

[12] Sapir, *Language*, 165–66.

meaning "to cut, scratch." Since writing, after its many metamorphoses, is still a process of making an impression upon a surface with a pointed instrument, I would say that the original denotative meaning survives. These are examples out of ordinary vocabulary showing that while processes may change, the essential idea of the process may be conserved in the word used to signify it. This sort of change does not play havoc with codes of behavior or institutions.

But I think we can recognize two types of semantic change that are inspired either by false reasoning or by motives that are objectionable. The first of them I shall call "rhetorical substitution"; the second, "rhetorical prevarication." (I leave out of account those changes that are the result of simple ignorance of lexical meaning on the part of a few, such as the use of "fortuitous" to mean "fortunate" or of "thus" to mean "therefore.")

The first of the improper changes keeps the old word but applies it to a new thing (the user not being aware that in the world of language words create "things.") Evidently, this has its source in the old iconic fallacy. One finds in the writings of modern semanticists a persistent tendency to refer to language as a "map" of what it stands for.[13] I say that this seems to go back to the iconic theory of meaning because a map is a small-scale configuration of the territory it plots. Language, on this supposition, must follow the outline of what it symbolizes. Now if a territory changes (e.g., if a river alters its course), the map has to change too. Otherwise, there will be a growing disparity between map and terrain, between language and the realities of the world, and we shall end in hallucinations. Words whose referents no longer exist are of no more use than outdated

[13] Irving J. Lee, *Language Habits in Human Affairs* (New York, 1941), 17–22.

maps. Always, of course, the referent, as a shaper of meaning, is supposed to be something "out there." But since the word continues to exist (and since it may have agreeable overtones), the trick is to take it and apply it to a new situation. One writer revealingly calls this adjusting language to "life facts."[14]

I believe it can be demonstrated that this is what has happened to the word "liberalism." In the nineteenth century, this word referred to an ideal of maximum individual liberty and minimum state interference, to put it generally. Today, it is being used to refer to something like the ideal of the welfare state, which involves many restrictions upon liberty. Now if those who use the word thus could be brought into a semantic disputation, I think they would argue that the new meaning is justified because the old meaning is no longer possible. And if we pushed them to explain why it is no longer possible, I think they would answer that "circumstances have changed." I would want to ask them next what changed circumstances have to do with an ideal construct. What they have done is to take the old term "liberalism," whose meaning polarized around a concept of personal liberty, and to use this to mean something like philanthropic activity through the machinery of the state. The two ideas are manifestly discrete, but they have used the word for the second idea because it carries with it some of the value connotations of the old one. The second idea is, according to them, the only context in which a benevolent man can now operate. In fact, however, liberalism in the old sense is still there as a viable ideal if the mind is disposed to receive that ideal. When they say that the old meaning is no longer possible in the circum-

[14] *Ibid.*, 83.

stances, what they are really indicating is that they prefer the new circumstances. Then they make the substitution, in disregard of the transcendental basis of language.

I believe that this is a very general truth. When a person blames a change of meaning upon changed facts, he is yielding to the facts and using them to justify a change that should not be made except by "ideal" consent. He is committing the fallacy of supposing that the reason for such change can lie outside the realm of discourse itself—that meaning must somehow tag along after empirical reality. All of this seems to reflect a purely materialist or "physicalist" view of the world. But if one believes that physical reality is the sole determinant of all things, including meanings, one collapses the relationship between what is physical and what is symbolic of meaning and value. It is another evidence of how the modern mind is trying to surrender its constitutive powers to the objective physical world.

The second kind of improper change, rhetorical prevarication, does not allege the excuse that the world has changed. It is a simple attempt to impose a change in the interest of an ideology. (I here use "ideology" in contradistinction to "philosophy." A philosophy, having a much wider circumspection, will have something to say about a word's meaning that connects with the larger work of the imagination. An ideology works to serve particular ends, and therefore the changes in meaning that it produces will not be circumspective and must result in a degree of injustice.) For example, when the modern leftist applies the term "reactionary" to everyone who will not accept the Marxist concept of economic and social organization, I would regard this as an ideological perversion. The Marxist is using the word to ascribe an impulse to "go backward" to people whose political views may reflect nothing more than a nonmaterialistic concept of man.

My next example is a more insidious and, therefore, more dangerous instance of prevarication. We mark a growing tendency among certain groups of people to refer to alcoholics, moral delinquents, and even criminals as "sick" people. The violence that this does to the legitimate meaning of "sick" is easily seen. We have always thought of a sick person as a man who is a victim of things beyond his control and who, therefore, deserves sympathy and assistance from his family and perhaps from society. If he becomes exposed to bacteria, which, of course, he cannot see, and contracts a disease, or if he suffers from some degeneration of tissue or bone, we regard him as undergoing a misfortune to which he did not in any conscious way contribute. He may become more or less a burden to his family and society, but not through any act of will.

Now the attempt is being made through this rhetorical prevarication to edge the delinquent and the criminal into this category. The result, it is almost too obvious to point out, is to remove the idea of moral responsibility from delinquency and crime. It has always been thought that society is the victim of the criminal. But now it is being implied, through a tendentious use of language, that the criminal is the victim of society, which did not take appropriate steps to keep him from getting "sick." By this verbal trick, what was formerly considered worthy of punishment is held up for indulgent sympathy.

This line of false reasoning probably begins with sentimentality. It certainly ends by denying the power of self-discipline. For what it says is this absurdity: Every man is conditioned, but the criminal is more conditioned than others; as a result, we are supposed to pity him and show him more solicitude than the person who is behaving himself and working hard at his job. Society has not agreed, and it cannot agree and maintain its own health, that those who have willfully done wrong belong in the same category and should be treated with the same commiseration as those who are afflicted with physical illness. It is, therefore, nothing less than scandalous to spread the view that alcoholics, criminals, and others who have adopted evil courses are merely "sick" people.

But to return to my earlier characterization: This is a designing shift, a deliberate misapplication in the interest of a special program. The users do not fall back on the excuse that reality has changed and that verbal usage must change with it; they simply take the word out of one context and put it in another in order to advance an ideological point of view. The ideology that is seeking to advance this prevarication is utterly hostile to the idea of freedom and the concomitant fact of responsibility. Such perversions have to be fought by a noetic and dialectical examination of the contents of the words involved.

This essay has attempted to relate the modern concept of relativism to language and, more particularly, to semantic reference. I shall emphasize, in closing, that the findings must be read in the light of one very important distinction. There is a difference between saying that language is relative because it is a convention and saying that because it is a convention it may be treated or used relativistically. If language is a more or less local convention, then its meanings are relative to those who use it. It clearly does not follow from this, however, that those who speak it may use it with unrestricted license. Here one might usefully paraphrase a statement that Burke makes about civil government: "If language is the product of convention, then that convention is its law." Now, when we say that that convention is its law, we accept the idea of prescriptive meaning. I would prefer to describe the fact with a word of stronger implication: language is a covenant among those who use it. It is in the nature of a covenant to be more than a matter of simple convenience, to be departed from for light and transient causes. A covenant—and I like, in this connection, the religious overtones of the word—binds us at deeper levels and involves some kind of confrontation of reality. When we covenant with one another that a word shall stand for a certain thing, we signify that it is the best available word for that thing in the present state of general understanding. The possibilities of refinement toward a more absolute correctness of meaning lie within and behind that convention. But as long as the convention is in effect, it has to be respected like any other rule, and this requires that departures from it must justify themselves.

Language, therefore, must be viewed as nonrelative in two ways. Meanings cannot be judged as relative simply to time and place; hence, in our dialectical vocabulary there is a theoretical absolute rightness of meaning. (Another distinction, which I owe to the members of this Symposium, is the difference between knowing an absolute and knowing an absolute absolutely. We posit, without knowing, an absolute correctness of meaning; how we attain toward that I have indicated in my remarks on poetry and imagination.) In the second place, the convention or covenant of language must be treated as absolutely binding upon us, as far as our human condition permits, until a change is authorized by right reason. These two considerations prevent the anarchy which an unconditional permissiveness— itself a pernicious absolute—would allow. They are all the defense that is needed for those who believe that both effective and right ways of saying things can be taught the student who is entering the universe of linguistic discourse.

What I am trying to say is that rhetoric is an essential ingredient of social cohesion; that an overstress upon dialectic saps rhetoric and that such overstress is precisely what we are getting today. . . . Concealed Rhetoric was presented before a symposium at Sea Island, Georgia, last September . . .

—RICHARD M. WEAVER TO RALPH T. EUBANKS
September 2, 1959

"Concealed Rhetoric" probes perceptively the relationship between "scientific objectivity" and "deliberative oratory" as exemplified in the work of the contemporary social scientist. Weaver indicts the social scientist who masquerades as the pure dialectician. To Weaver social science employs the method of the rhetorician and should therefore be called "social philosophy," thus enabling the discipline to free itself from the positivistic limitations of science and to practice honestly the art of the "noble rhetorician."

Kenneth Burke's influence is herein reflected in Weaver's discussion of positive and dialectical terms and in his description of rhetoric as "a process of making . . . identification." Yet Weaver has put his own stamp upon Burke's concept in this acute interpretation of the role of "name-calling" in identification. He thus fuses Burkean "identification" with his own concept of "the ethical rhetoric," producing a biting indictment of the social scientist as "dialectician . . . without a dialectical basis."

Concealed Rhetoric
in Scientistic Sociology

THIS INQUIRY concerns some problems posed by the use of rhetoric in the dissemination of a professedly scientific knowledge of man. It assumes that rhetoric in its right character is one of the useful arts, and that knowledge about the nature and behavior of man can be gained and should be propagated as widely as possible. The question of what things should precede and enter into that dissemination, however, continues to raise real perplexities. Many of us who read the literature of social science as laymen are conscious of being admitted at a door which bears the watchword "scientific objectivity" and of emerging at another door which looks out upon a variety of projects for changing, renovating, or revolutionizing society. In consequence, we feel the need of a more explicit account of how the student of society passes from facts to values or statements of policy.

I would reject at the outset any assumption that the man

who studies social phenomena either could or should be incapable of indignation and admiration. Such a person, were it possible for him to exist, would have a very limited function, and it is hard to see how he could be a wise counselor about the matters with which he deals. It seems probable that no one would ever devote himself to the study of society unless he had some notion of an "ought," or of the way he would like to see things go. The real focus of this study is on the point at which social science and rhetoric meet and on the question of whether this meeting, in the case of what will here be labelled "scientistic" sociology, has resulted in deception rather than in open and legitimate argument. To begin the inquiry, it will be necessary to say a few things about the nature of rhetoric.

I. RHETORICAL AND SCIENTIFIC DISCOURSE

Rhetoric is anciently and properly defined as the art of persuasion. We may deduce from this that it is essentially concerned with producing movement, which may take the form of a change of attitude or the adoption of a course of action, or both. This art, whether it presents itself in linguistic or in other form (and I would suggest that a bank or other business corporation which provides itself with a tall and imposing looking building is demonstrating that there is even a rhetoric of matter or of scene) meets the person to whom it is addressed and takes him where the rhetor wishes him to go, even if that "going" is nothing more than an intensification of feeling about something. This means that rhetoric, consciously employed, is never innocent of intention, but always has as its object the exerting of some kind of compulsion.

Defining rhetoric thus as the art of persuasion does not,

however, divorce it entirely from scientific knowledge. My view is that the complete rhetorician is the man of knowledge who has learned, in addition to his knowledge, certain arts of appeal which have to do with the inspiring of feeling. Indeed, the scientist and the rhetorician both begin with an eye on the nature of things. A rhetoric without a basis in science is inconceivable, because people are moved to action by how they "read" the world or the phenomena of existence, and science is the means of representing these in their existential bearings. People respond according to whether they believe that certain things exist with fixed natures, or whether they accept as true certain lines of cause-and-effect relationship, or whether they accept as true certain other relationships, such as the analogical. One might, speaking as a scientist, define man as an animal, or he might assert that government spending is a cause of inflation, or he might assert that war and murder are similar kinds of things. But one could also make these statements as a rhetorician. How, then, can one distinguish between the two kinds of statements?

The difference is that science is a partial universe of discourse, which is concerned only with facts and the relationships between them. Rhetoric is concerned with a wider realm, since it must include both the scientific occurrence and the axiological ordering of these facts. For the rhetorician the tendency of the statement is the primary thing, because it indicates his position or point of view in his universe of discourse. Rhetorical presentation always carries perspective. The scientific inquirer, on the other hand, is merely noting things as they exist in empirical conjunction. He is not passing judgment on them because his presentment, as long as it remains scientific, is not supposed to be anything more than classificatory. The statement of a scientist that "man is an animal" is intended only to locate man in a biological group as a result of empirical finding; but the rhetorician's statement of the same thing is not the same in effect. For him the term "animal" is not a mere positive designation, but a term loaded with tendency from the wider context in which he is using it. He is endeavoring to get a response by identifying man with a class of beings toward which a certain attitude is predictable. He has taken the term out of the positive vocabulary and made it dialectical, a distinction I shall take up presently.

It may now be suggested that if the sociologists whom I am here calling "scientistic" had been true scientists, they would have asked at the beginning, what is the real classification of the subject of their study? And having answered that, they would have asked next, what is the mode of inquiry most appropriate to that study? I am assuming that the answers to their questions would have told them that their subject matter is largely subjective, that much of it is not susceptible of objective or quantitative measurement, and that all or nearly all of their determinations would be inextricably bound up with considerations of value. This would have advised them that however scientific they might try to be in certain of their procedures—as in the analysis of existing facts—the point would be reached where they would have to transcend these and group their facts in categories of significance and value.

But what some of the more influential of them did was decide that the phenomena which they were engaged in studying were the same as those which the physical scientists were studying with such impressive results and that the same methods and much of the same terminology would be appropriate to the prosecution of that study.

II. THE ORIGINAL RHETORICAL MANEUVER

My thesis is that in making this decision they were acting not as scientists but as rhetoricians, because they were trying to capitalize on a prestige and share in an approbation, to the disregarding of the nature of the subject they were supposed to be dealing with. Sociology took this turn at a time when the prestige of physical science was very great, possibly greater than it is even today, since certain limitations had not then been encountered or fully considered. Physical science was beginning to change the face of the earth, and it was adding greatly to the wealth-producing machinery of mankind. It was very human for a group engaged in developing a body of knowledge to wish to hitch its wagon to that star. F. A. Hayek, in *The Counter-Revolution of Science,* has related the case as follows: "Their [the physical scientists'] success was such that they came to exert an extraordinary fascination on those working in other fields, who rapidly began to imitate their teaching and vocabulary. . . . These [subjects] became increasingly concerned to vindicate their equal status by showing that their methods were the same as those of their more brilliantly successful sisters rather than by adapting their methods more and more to their own particular problems."

Accordingly, the founders of scientistic sociology did not so much arrive independently at a definition of sociology (in doing which they would have been scientists) as seek identification, for external reasons, with another field of study. In proceeding thus they were not trying to state the nature of their subject; they were trying to get a value imputed to it. That this was their original rhetorical maneuver can be shown in the following way.

Rhetoric can be visualized as altogether a process of making this kind of identification. The process is simply that of merging something we would like to see taken as true with something that is believed to be true, of something we would like to get accepted with something that is accepted. Such operation can be seen in the most rudimentary of all rhetorical devices, which is sometimes termed "name calling." To something that we wish to see accepted, we apply a name carrying prestige; to something that we wish to see rejected, we apply a name that is distasteful. Rhetoric thus works through eulogistic and dyslogistic vocabularies. It is the thing-to-be-identified-with that provides the impulse, whether favorable or unfavorable. The honest and discriminating rhetorician chooses these things with regard to reason and a defensible scheme of values; the dishonest or unthinking one may seize upon any terms which seem to possess impulse, just to make use of their tractive power.

If the foregoing analysis is correct, the scientistic sociologists applied a prestige-carrying name to their study. They were not classifying in the true sense; they were instigating an attitude. In brief, "social science" is itself a rhetorical expression, not an analytical one. The controversy over their methods and recommendations which goes on today continues to reflect that fact.

III. POSITIVE AND DIALECTICAL TERMS

Having thus assumed the role of scientists, they were under a necessity of maintaining that role. And this called for further "identifications." Perhaps the most mischievous of these has been the collapsing of the distinction between positive and dialectical terms. Since this distinction is of the first importance to those who would deal with these matters critically, I shall try to make clear what is meant by it.

Practically everyone grants that not all of the terms in our vocabulary refer to the same kind of thing. The difference between those which refer to positive entities and those which refer to dialectical ones is of decisive significance for the investigator. "Positive" terms stand for observable objects capable of physical identification and measurement. They are terms whose referents are things existing objectively in the world, whose presence supposedly everyone can be brought to acknowledge. "Rock," "tree," and "house" are examples. Positive terms thus make up a "physicalist" vocabulary, inasmuch as they represent the objects of sensory perception (even when these have to be noted by dials and meters). Properly speaking, there cannot be an argument about a positive term; there can be only a dispute, which is subject to settlement by actual observation or measurement.

"Dialectical" terms come from a different source, because they take their meaning from the world of idea and action. They are words for essences and principles, and their meaning is reached not through sensory perception, but through the logical processes of definition, inclusion, exclusion, and implication. Since their meaning depends on a concatenation of ideas, what they signify cannot be divorced from the ideological position of the user as revealed by the general context of his discourse. A scientist, as we have noted, locates things in their empirical conjunction, but the user of dialectic must locate the meaning of his entities in the logical relationships of his system, and hence his discovery of them cannot be an empirical discovery. For this reason we say that the meaning of "justice" or "goodness" or "fair play" is not "found," but rather "arrived at." It is implied by the world of idea and attitude with which the user started. A dialectical term does not stand for "motion," as the positive term out of science might do, but for "action," which cannot be freed from the idea of purpose and value.

The scientistic sociologist has tried to maintain his scientific stance by endeavoring to give the impression that all the terms he uses are positive and hence can be used with the same "objectivity" and preciseness as those of the physical scientist. I say he has endeavored to give the impression, because even an impression that this can be done is difficult to induce for any length of time, as I believe the following examples will show.

Let us take for illustration an expression fairly common in sociological parlance today: "the underprivileged," and ask ourselves how one determines its meaning. We see at once that it is impossible to reach the meaning of "the underprivileged" without reference to the opposed term, "the privileged." Evidently one has first to form a concept of "the privileged," and this will be in reference to whatever possessions and opportunities are thought of as conferring privilege. The one term is arrived at through logical privation of the other, and neither is conceivable without some original idea frankly carrying evaluation. "Privilege" suggests of course something that people desire, and hence "the privileged" are those in whose direction we wish to move, and "the underprivileged" constitute the class we wish to escape from. But where is the Geiger counter with which we could go out into society and locate one of the underprivileged? We would have to use some definition of privilege, arising out of an original inclination toward this or that ideal.

Or, let us take the more general expression "social problem." How is one to become aware of the supposedly objective fact or facts denoted by this expression? According to one sociologist, a social problem is "any situation which attracts the attention of a considerable number of competent observers within a society and appeals to them as calling for readjustment or remedy by social, *i.e.*, collective, action of some kind or other." At least three items in this definition warn us that a social problem is not something that just anybody could identify, like an elephant in a parade, but something that must be determined by a dialectical operation. First of all, the observer must be competent, which I take to mean trained not just in seeing objective things, but in knowing when ideas or values are threatened by their opposites. This perception appeals to him for an attitude to be followed by an action, and moreover this action must be of the putatively most beneficial kind, "social" or "collective."

The point I wish to make here is that the scientistic sociologist is from the very beginning caught up in a plot, as it were, of attitude and action, and that he cannot divorce the meaning of the incidents from the structure of the plot. The plot is based on a position which takes facts out of empirical conjunction and places them in logical or dialectical constructions.

He is therefore not dealing in positive words that have a single fixed meaning when he uses terms that depend on a context for their signification. Another way of expressing this is to say that the terms in his vocabulary are polar, in that their meaning changes according to what they are matched with. And since the sociologist has the opportu-

nity to match them with almost anything, he is not dealing
with scientific invariables when he talks about "the underprivileged" or "a social problem." He is being an ethical
philosopher from the beginning, with the responsibility
which that implies.

The conclusion comes down to this: things which are
discriminated empirically cannot thereafter by the same
operation be discriminated dialectically. If one wishes to
arrive at a dialectical discrimination, one has to start from a
position which makes that possible.

IV. OTHER FORMS OF "IDENTIFICATION"

This ignoring of the nature of dialectical inquiry is the
most serious perversion committed by the scientificists in
seeking to maintain their identification, but there are other,
perhaps more superficial, procedures, whose general end is
the same kind of simulation. One of the more noticeable is
what might be called pedantic analysis. The scientistic
sociologist wishes people to feel that he is just as empirical
and thoroughgoing as the natural scientist, and that his
conclusions are based just as relentlessly on observed data.
The desire to present this kind of facade accounts, one may
suspect, for the many examples and the extensive use of
statistical tables found in the works of some of them. It has
been said of certain novelists that they create settings having such a wealth of realistic detail that the reader assumes
that the plot which is to follow will be equally realistic,
when this may be far from the case. What happens is that
the novelist disarms the reader with the realism of his
setting in order that he may "get away with murder" in his
plot. The persuasiveness of the scene is thus counted on to

spill over into the action of the story. In like manner, when a treatise on social science is filled with this kind of data, the realism of the latter can influence our acceptance of the thesis, which may, on scrutiny, rest on very dubious constructs, such as definitions of units.

Along with this there is sometimes a great display of scientific preciseness in formulations. But my reading suggests that some of these writers are often very precise about matters which are not very important and rather imprecise about matters which are. Most likely this is an offsetting process. If there are subjects one cannot afford to be precise about because they are too little understood or because one's views of them are too contrary to traditional beliefs about society, one may be able to maintain an appearance of scientific correctness by taking great pains in the expressing of matters of little consequence. These will afford scope for a display of scholarly meticulousness and of one's command of the scientific terminology.

At the opposite extreme, but intended for the same effect, is the practice of being excessively tentative in the statement of conclusions and generalizations. The natural scientists have won an enviable reputation for modesty in this respect; they seldom allow their desire for results to carry them beyond a statement of what is known or seriously probable. This often calls for a great deal of qualification, so that cautious qualification has become the hallmark of the scientific method. It is my impression, however, that a good many modern sociologists do their qualifying not for the purpose of protecting the truth but of protecting themselves. There is a kind of qualification which is mere hedging. I offer as an example a sentence from an article entitled "Some Neglected Aspects of the Problem of Poverty." The author begins his definition thus: "It would seem that it is nothing more nor less than a comparative social condition depending on a relative control over economic goods, the standard of comparison being a group possessing a maximum of such control, called the rich or wealthy." There appear at the very beginning of this sentence two important qualifiers: (1) the verb is thrown into a conditional mode by the use of the auxiliary "would," and (2) the verb is not the categorical "is" but the tentative "seem," with its suggestion that one may be dealing only with appearances. This is followed by "nothing more nor less," which is a purely rhetorical flourish, evidently intended to make us feel that the author is going to be definite, whereas he has just advised us that he is not. What looks like carefulness is mere evasiveness; this writer does not want to assume the risk of saying what poverty is. Instances of such unwillingness to make a firm declaratory statement are so numerous that they almost constitute the style of a type of social science writing. With the unwary reader, unfortunately, this style may encourage confidence, whereas it should lead to challenge.

V. APPEALS TO AUTHORITY

In addition to a language simulating that of science, the scientistic sociologists make use of an external means of persuasion in the form of appeal to authority. A common practice with some of these writers when they are dealing with a subject that is controversial or involved with value judgments is to cite an impressive array of authorities. There is nothing improper in itself, of course, about the invoking of authority. But when we look at the method of certain of these authors, we are likely to find that the authorities are other social scientists who happen to share the particular view which is being presented. What looks like an inductive survey of opinions may in fact be a selection of *ex parte* pronouncements. Still, such marshalling of authorities, often accompanied by a quotation from each to heighten the sense of reality or conviction, can easily give the impression that all authority is behind the view being advanced. Thus many textbooks on social problems bristle with the names of persons whose claims to authority may be quite unknown to the reader, but whose solemn citation may be depended on to exert a persuasive force. One suspects that it is the appearance rather than the real pertinence of the authority which is desired.

Along with this there is another, and a more subtle, kind of appeal to authority which takes the form of a patter of modern shibboleths. These may be out of fairly everyday language, but they will be words and expressions associated with leaders of opinion, with current intellectual fashions, with big projects, and with things in general which are supposed to have a great future. Professor A. H. Hobbs, in his *Social Problems and Scientism*, lists among others: *modern, rational, liberal, professional, intergovernmental, objectivity, research, disciplines, workshops, interrelations, human resources*, and *human development*. I would suggest that this language represents an appeal to the authority of the "modern mind." These are expressions carrying a certain melioristic bias, which one will have difficulty in resisting without putting oneself in the camp of reaction or obscurantism. The repeated use of them has the effect of setting up a kind of incantation, so that to sound in dissonance with them is virtually to brand oneself as anti-social. The reader is left with the alternative of accepting them and of going along on assumptions he does not approve of, or of rejecting them, which would entail continuous argument and would involve taking a position almost impossible to explain to a "modern."

The use of appeals based on authority brings up again the role of the sociologist as advocate.

At the beginning of his treatise on *Rhetoric* Aristotle divides the art into three kinds: deliberative, forensic, and epideictic. Epideictic rhetoric is devoted to celebrating (as in the panegyric); forensic rhetoric is concerned with the justice or injustice of things which have already happened; and deliberative oratory is concerned with the future, since the speaker is urging his audience to do, or to refrain from doing, something or other. "The end of the deliberative speaker is the expedient or the harmful; for he who exhorts recommends a course of action as better, and he who dissuades advises against it as worse; all other considerations, such as justice and injustice, honor and disgrace, are included as accessory in relation to this." By the terms of this definition a considerable part of sociological writing must be classified as deliberative oratory, and the practitioners of it as rhetoricians. When one sets up to advise concerning alternative social courses, one does exactly what the ancient orator in Areopagus or forum was doing, however much the abstractness of one's language may tend to conceal that fact. As Kenneth Burke has pointed out: ". . . when you begin talking about the optimum rate of speed at which cultural change should take place or the optimum proportion between tribal and individualistic motives which should prevail under a given set of economic conditions, you are talking about something very important indeed; but you will find yourself deep in matters of rhetoric, for nothing is more rhetorical in nature than a deliberation as to what is too much or too little, too early or too late. . . ."

A good many current texts on sociology are replete with this kind of deliberation. Martin Neumeyer, in his *Social Problems and the Changing Society*, while discussing numerous opinions on the topics with which he deals, often steps into the role of judge and advocate. Thus we read: "Homicides, suicides, illegitimate births, deaths due to venereal disease and the like seem to be more prevalent where there is low integration in cities. The more adequately a city provides for the health and welfare of its citizens, the greater the chance of preventing or controlling deviations. Well integrated cities are likely to have a better chance of survival and growth than poorly integrated urban areas." It might be contended that this passage is merely descriptive of certain laws of social phenomena. Still, the presence of such phrases as "more adequately," "health and welfare of its citizens," and "a better chance of survival and growth" show plainly that the passage is written from a standpoint of social meliorism.

The same kind of thing is done by George Lundberg, in his *Foundations of Sociology*, when he becomes a pleader on the subject of language itself. He argues that we ought to give up those terms created by the original myth and metaphor-making disposition of the human mind in favor of a different "symbolic equipment." That he is entirely willing to utilize traditional rhetoric in making his point may be seen from the following passage: "Untold nervous energy, time, and natural resources are wasted in warfare upon or protection against entirely imaginary monsters conjured up by words. Widespread mental disorders result from constantly finding the world different from the word-maps upon which we rely for guidance and adjustment. Social problems cannot be solved as long as they are stated in terms as primitive and unrealistic as those which attributed disease to demons and witches."

A feature of another kind indicating that a good many sociologists are engaged in more or less concealed deliberative oratory is the presence in their work of a large amount of enthymematic reasoning. Reasoning in this form is a rhetorical kind of convincing, and the enthymeme is actually described by Aristotle as the "rhetorical syllogism." In the textbooks of logic it is defined as a syllogism with one of the propositions withheld. In the argument

> All who are patriots should be willing to
> sacrifice for their country
> You should be willing to sacrifice for your
> country

it is seen that the minor premise, "You are a patriot," is missing. It has been omitted because the maker of the argument has assumed that it is granted by the hearer and will be supplied by him to complete the argument.

This type of argument is rightly described as rhetorical because the rhetorician always gets his leverage by starting with the things that are accepted. By combining these with things he wants to get accepted ("identification" again) he moves on to the conclusion which is his object. In other words, because the rhetorician can assume certain things— because he does not have to demonstrate every proposition in his argument—he can work from statements which are essentially appeals. He studies beforehand the disposition of his auditors and takes note of those beliefs which will afford him firm ground—those general convictions about which one does not have to be deliberative. Hence the enthymeme is rhetorical, as distinguished from the syllogism, because it capitalizes on something already in the mind of the hearer. The speaker tacitly assumes one position, and from this he can move on to the next.

A number of contemporary sociologists, as I read them, use the enthymeme for the purpose of getting accepted a proposition which could be challenged on one ground or another. They make an assumption regarding the nature or goals of society and treat this as if it were universally granted and therefore not in need of explicit assertion. I refer again to Neumeyer's *Social Problems and the Changing Society*. This work seems to rest its case on an enthymeme which, if expanded to a complete syllogism, would go on as follows:

> If society is democratic and dynamic, these
> prescriptions are valid
> Society is democratic and dynamic
> Therefore these prescriptions are valid

What the author does in effect is withhold his minor premise apparently on the ground that no man of sense and information will question it. Therefore he does not take seriously those who would ask, "Is society really democratic and dynamic?" or "In what ways is society democratic and dynamic?" (What is to take care of societies which are aristocratic and traditional, or do they have no social problems?) Having thus assumed the premise he needs in order to get his conclusion, he can proceed to describe the techniques which would be proper in a democratic and dynamic society as if they were the only ones to be taken into account.

There is nothing illicit about enthymematic arguments; they are to be encountered frequently wherever argumentation occurs. My point is that something significant is implied by their presence here. Even if we are clear as to why the sociologist must argue, why is he employing a form of argument recognized as "rhetorical"?

This takes us back to the original question regarding his province and specifically to the relationship of what he does to the world of value. A good many current writers in the field seem rather coy on the subject of values; they admit that the problem of value has to be faced; but then they merely circle about it and leave specific values to shift for themselves. (Occasionally one takes a more definite stand, as when Francis E. Merrill declares that the values of a social scientist are the values given him by virtue of his membership in a democratic and progressive society.) Even so respected a thinker as Max Weber seems less than satisfactory on the two roles of the social scientist. His position is that "the distinction between the purely logically deducible and empirical factual assertions on the one hand, and practical, ethical, or philosophical judgments on the other hand is correct, but that nevertheless . . . both problems belong within the area of instruction." Obviously the problem is how to encompass both of them. What Weber does is lay down a rule for academic objectivity. The teacher must set "as his unconditional duty, in every single case, even to the point where it involves the danger of making his lectures less lively or less attractive, to make relentlessly clear to his audience, and especially to himself, which of his statements are statements of logically deduced or empirically related facts and which are statements of practical evaluations."

My question would be how the sociologist can in good conscience leave the first to embark upon the second without having something in the nature of a philosophy of society. His dilemma is that he is perforce a dialectician, but he is without a dialectical basis. He must use dialectical terms, but he has no framework which will provide a consistent extra-empirical reference for them, though we may feel sometimes that we can see one trying to force itself through, as in the concept of society's essence as something "democratic and progressive." It seems to me that the dilemma could be faced with more candor and realism. No practical man will deny that the student of society can make use of many of the findings of positive science. Things must be recognized in their brute empirical existence; we are constantly running into things of which we were unaware until they proclaimed their objectivity by impinging upon our senses. And there are some things which must be counted. A pure subjective idealism is a luxury which may be afforded by a few thinkers, but it is not a prudential system. I for one can hardly believe that science is purely ancillary in the sense of finding evidence for what we already believe or wish to believe. The world is too independent a datum for that.

On the other hand, a large part of the subject matter of the student of society does consist of the subjective element in human beings. This has to be recognized as a causative agent. History shows many opinions, highly erroneous or fantastic, which have been active influences on human behavior. This factor has to be studied, but it cannot be simplistically quantified. Here as least there must be room for speculative inquiry.

Finally, the student of society should realize that he is a man writing as a man. He cannot free himself entirely from perspective. His view of things can have a definite bearing on what is regarded as a fact or on how factual units can be employed. To argue that the social scientist should adopt no perspective on matters is perhaps in itself to adopt a perspective, but a far less fruitful one than those in which, with proper regard for objective facts, a viewpoint is frankly espoused.

In view of these considerations, why does not social science call itself "social philosophy"? This would widen its universe of discourse, freeing it from the positivistic limitations of science and associating its followers with the love of wisdom. At the same time it would enable them to practice the art of noble rhetoric where it is called for, without unconscious deception and without a feeling that they are compromising their profession.

I am struggling along with a book MS long in arrears. Perhaps I should mention that one chapter of this book is entitled "The Cultural Role of Rhetoric." In this I try to prove the proposition that in the social realm dialectic unaided by rhetoric is subversive. Then I try to show that Modern (or General) Semantics is a modern attempt to exalt pure dialectic at the expense of traditional rhetoric, and that this is one of the things eating away the fibre of our society.

—RICHARD M. WEAVER TO RALPH T. EUBANKS
September 2, 1959

"Speech," Weaver argued in *Ideas Have Consequences*, "is the vehicle of order." He later developed this premise as the major thesis of "The Cultural Role of Rhetoric." In his view, rhetoric is the *vital* force in the maintenance of the internal order of spirit and the external order of society. In the explication of this view, Weaver associated rhetoric with "memory" and with "sentiment." Rhetoric, he insisted, deals with questions that "arise out of history."

It is rhetoric, therefore, which "speaks to man in his whole being and out of his whole past and with reference to values which only a human being can intuit." Here then is a cardinal tenet of Weaver's credo: rhetoric conceived as the "most humanistic of all the disciplines." Thus it was that he assigned to rhetoric a special role in resolving the cultural crisis of our time. In Weaver's "restored man" dialectic and rhetoric would go hand in hand "as the regime of human faculties intended they should."

The Cultural Role
of Rhetoric

ONE OF THE most alarming results of the disparagement of memory is the tide of prejudice which is currently running against rhetoric. Everyone is aware that the old-style orator is no more, and even those speeches which suggest traditional oratory arouse skepticism and suspicion. The discourse that is favored today is without feeling and resonance, so that it is no exaggeration to say that eloquence itself has fallen into disfavor. Moments of great crisis do indeed encourage people to listen for a while to a Churchill or a MacArthur, and this is proof of the indispensability of rhetoric when men feel that great things are at stake. But today when the danger is past, they lapse again into their dislike of the rhetorical mode, labeling all discourse which has discernible emotional appeal "propaganda."

Rhetoric is involved along with memory in this trend because rhetoric depends upon history. All questions that are susceptible to rhetorical treatment arise out of history, and it is to history that the rhetorician turns for his means of persuasion. Now simultaneous with the loss of historical consciousness there emerges a conviction that man should dispense with persuasive speech and limit himself to mere communication. Viewed in the long perspective this must be considered a phase of the perennial issue between rhetoric and dialectic. But great danger lies in the fact that the present attitude represents a victory for a false conception of the role of dialectic in cultural life. States and societies cannot be secure unless there is in their public expression a partnership of dialectic and rhetoric. Dialectic is abstract reasoning upon the basis of propositions; rhetoric is the relation of the terms of these to the existential world in which facts are regarded with sympathy and are treated with that kind of historical understanding and appreciation which lie outside the dialectical process.

The current favor which rational and soulless discourse enjoys over rhetoric is a mask for the triumph of dialectic. This triumph is directly owing to the great prestige of modern science. Dialectic must be recognized as a counterpart in expression in language of the activity of science. We can affirm this, despite certain differences between them, because they are both rational and they are both neutral. The first point we need not labor; the second is important for this discussion because it is the quality of neutrality in science which has caused many moderns to suppose that it should be the model for linguistic discourse.

We hear it regularly asserted that the investigations and conclusions of science are not made to serve *ad hoc* causes. It is usually granted that the scientist is indifferent to the potencies which he makes available. His work is finished when he can say, "Here are these potencies." He is a solver of intellectual problems, as is evidenced by his reliance upon number.

Now, in a fashion similar enough to make the resemblance consequential, the dialectician is neutral toward the bearing of his reasoning upon actuality. The dialectician says, "If you assume these propositions, you must face these implications," and so forth. His work is with logical inference, not historical discovery. If we define dialectic in its pure form, we are compelled to say that it is indifferent to truth, or at least that its truth is something contained in its own operation. Professor Mortimer Adler has pointed out that "truth when it is taken to mean an extrinsic relation of thinking to entities beyond the process of thought cannot be achieved by dialectical thinking."[1] What is said here assumes the possibility of a pure dialectician, and it may be doubted, because of the nature of things, that such a person could exist. But the question I am here pursuing is whether one can become too committed to dialectic for his own good and the good of those whom he influences. I expect to show presently through a famous instance how this can happen.

My thesis is that a too exclusive reliance upon dialectic is a mistake of the most serious consequence because *dialectic alone in the social realm is subversive.* The widespread overturning of institutions in recent history and the frustration man now feels over his inability to guide his destiny begin, at the most profound level, with the disastrous notion that dialectic, unaided by rhetoric, is sufficient for human counsels. We have heard it contended by many leaders of opinion that if man will only avoid emotional

---

[1] Mortimer Adler, *Dialectic* (New York, 1927), 31.

approaches and will utilize science in coping with his problems, he will be able to conduct his affairs with a success
hitherto unknown. That is to say, if he will rely upon a
dialectic which is a counterpart to that of science in arriv-
ing at his decisions, he will have the advantage of pure
knowledge whereas in the past he has tried to get along
with a mass of knowledge and feeling. The point of this
chapter will be the contrary: to give up the role of rhetoric
and to trust all to dialectic is a fast road to social subver-
sion.

For the introduction of this argument I am going back to
the trial and condemnation of Socrates. Certain features of
this extraordinary incident will help to illuminate the difficult problem of the relation of dialectic to rhetoric and of
both of these to practical policy.

The reflective portion of mankind has wondered for centuries how so brilliant and civilized a people as the Greeks
could condemn to death this famous philosopher. It would
be blasphemous for anyone to suggest that the Athenian
assembly did not commit a dreadful injustice. But since the
condemnation occurred, there must have been some cause;
and I think the cause lies much deeper than the fact that a
few men with whom Socrates associated turned out badly
and deeper than the resentment of a few Athenians whose
vanity he had wounded through his questioning. The people of Athens had a case against Socrates which can be
understood and elucidated. Set against their own attitudes
and behavior, the case may not look very good to us, and
we can still say that they put to death the most virtuous
man in the city. Yet they had a certain cause, possibly more
felt than reasoned out, but enough to account practically
for the final judgment.

Socrates has come down to us as one of the greatest

ethical teachers of all times. But by the Athenians who indicted him he was charged with being a subverter and a corrupter. Before we set down these two ascriptions as wholly incompatible, let us remember that Socrates was also the greatest dialectician of his time. We who study him at this remote date are chiefly impressed with the ethical aspect of his teaching, but those who listened to him in Athens may have been more impressed by his method, which was that of dialectic. By turning his great dialectical skill upon persons and institutions, Socrates could well have produced the feeling that he was an enemy of the culture which the Greeks had created. He was, in one sense of course, the highest expression of it, but the kind of skill he brought to a peak of development needs harmonizing with other things. When a dialectic operates independently of the concrete facts of a situation, it can be destructive. These facts are not determinative logically of the course which the dialectical inquiry must take, but they are the ground from which it must operate in actual discourse. A dialectic which becomes irresponsibly independent shatters the matrix which provides the base for its operation. In this fact must have lain the real source of the hostility toward Socrates. Nietzsche has perceived this brilliantly in a passage of *The Birth of Tragedy*: "From this point onward Socrates conceives it his duty to correct existence; and with an air of irreverence and superiority, as the precursor of an altogether different culture, art, and morality, he enters single-handed into a world, to touch whose very hem would give us the greatest happiness."[2]

We must remember that Socrates begins the *Apology* by telling his auditors that they are not going to hear a clever

[2] *The Birth of Tragedy*, translated by Clifton Fadiman, *The Philosophy of Nietzsche*, V (5 vols.; Modern Library Edition: New York, 1937), 253.

speaker; that is to say, they are not going to hear an orator of the kind they are accustomed to; if Socrates is a good speaker, it is not in the style of his accusers. They have said nothing that is true; he proposes to speak only the truth. Further along, he professes to be "an utter foreigner to the manner of speech here." Obviously this is not the way in which a speaker consolidates himself with an audience; it betokens alienation rather than identification. Socrates has in effect said at the beginning, "Your way is not my way."

Thereafter Socrates gives an account of the origin of his unpopularity. He had gone around to men who were reputed to be wise and had questioned them about matters of which they were supposed to have knowledge. He found it easy to prove that they were not wise but ignorant or that their knowledge was so confined that it could scarcely be termed wisdom. Among those who underwent his examination were public men, or political leaders, and poets. This story is too well known to readers of the *Dialogues* to need rehearsing in detail. Suffice it to say that Socrates gives a candid relation of how his dialectic had irritated important elements in the population. But it is to the role of dialectic in the defense itself that I wish to direct chief attention. For Socrates, when his life was at stake, could not or would not give up the instrumentality by which he had been offending.

Let us look at the literal charge which has come down to us. "Socrates is a transgressor and a busybody, investigating things beneath the earth and in the heavens, and making the worse appear the better reason and teaching these things to others." Added to this was the further charge that he did not recognize the gods which were acknowledged by the state but insisted on introducing an idea of new spiritual beings. No doubt there are several ways in which this latter charge could have been answered. But the way in which Socrates chose to meet it was exactly the way to exacerbate the feelings of those whom he had earlier offended. It is significant that at one point he feels compelled to say to the assembly: "Please bear in mind not to make a disturbance if I conduct my argument in my accustomed manner." Here is the passage which follows that request:

SOCRATES: You say what is incredible, Melitus, and that, as appears to me, even to yourself. For this man, O Athenians! appears to me to be very insolent and intemperate, and to have preferred this indictment through downright insolence, intemperance, and wantonness. For he seems, as it were, to have composed an enigma for the purpose of making an experiment. Whether will Socrates the wise know that I am jesting, and contradict myself, or shall I deceive him and all who hear me. For, in my opinion, he clearly contradicts himself in the indictment, as if he should say, Socrates is guilty of wrong in not believing that there are gods, and in believing that there are gods. And this, surely, is the act of one who is trifling.

Consider with me now, Athenians, in what respect he appears to me to say so. And do you, Melitus, answer me, and do ye, as I besought you at the outset, remember not to make an uproar if I speak after my usual manner.

Is there any man, Melitus, who believes that there are human affairs, but does not believe that there are men? Let him answer, judges, and not make so much noise. Is there anyone who does not believe that there are horses, but that there are things pertaining to horses? or who does not believe that there are pipers, but that there are things pertaining to pipes? There is not, O best of men! For since you are not willing to answer, I say it to you and to all here present. But answer to this at least: is there anyone who believes that there are things relating to demons, but does not believe that there are demons?

MELITUS: There is not.

SOCRATES: How obliging you are in having hardly answered, though compelled by these judges! You assert, then, that I do believe and teach things relating to demons, whether they be new or old; therefore, according to your admission, I do believe in things relating to demons, and this you have sworn in the bill of indictment. If, then, I believe in things relating to demons, there is surely an absolute necessity that I should believe that there are demons. Is it not so? It is. For I suppose you assent, since you do not answer. But with respect to demons, do we not allow that they are gods, or the children of gods? Do you admit this or not?

MELITUS: Certainly.

SOCRATES: Since, then, I allow that there are demons, as you admit, if demons are a kind of gods, this is the point in which I say you speak enigmatically and divert yourself in saying that I do not allow there are gods, and again that I do allow there are, since I allow that there are demons? But if demons are the children of gods, spurious ones, either from nymphs or any others, of whom they are reported to be, what man can think that there are sons of gods, and yet that there are not gods? For it would be just as absurd if anyone would think that there are mules, the offspring of horses and asses, but should not think that there are horses and asses. However, Melitus, it cannot be otherwise than that you have preferred this indictment for the purpose of trying me, or because you were at loss what real crime to allege against me; for that you should persuade any man who has the smallest degree of sense that the same person can think there are things relating to demons and to gods, and yet that there are neither demons, nor gods, nor heroes, is utterly impossible.[3]

This shows in a clear way the weapon that Socrates had wielded against so many of his contemporaries. It is, in

[3] Henry Cary (trans.), *The Apology*, in *The Works of Plato*, I (6 vols.; London, 1858).

fact, a fine example of the dialectical method: first the establishment of a class; then the drawing out of implications; and finally the exposure of the contradiction. As far as pure logic goes, it is undeniably convincing; yet after all, this is not the way in which one talks about one's belief in the gods. The very rationality of it suggests some lack of organic feeling. It has about it something of the look of a trap or a trick, and one can imagine hearers not very sympathetic to the accused saying to themselves: "There is Socrates up to his old tricks again. That is the way he got into trouble. He is showing that he will never be any different." We may imagine that the mean and sullen Melitus, his interlocutor at this point—nothing good is intended of him here—was pleased rather than otherwise that Socrates was conducting himself so true to form. It underscored the allegations that were implied in the indictment.

This is not the only kind of argument offered by Socrates in his defense, it is true. In fact this particular argument is followed by a noble one based upon analogy, in which he declared that just as he would not desert the station he was commanded to guard while he was a soldier, so he would not give up his duty of being a gadfly to the men of Athens, which role he felt had been assigned him by the gods. Yet there is in the *Apology*, as a whole, enough of the clever dialectician—of the man who is concerned merely with logical inferences—to bring to the minds of the audience the side of Socrates which had aroused enmity.

The issue comes to a focus on this: Socrates professed to be a teacher of virtue, but his method of teaching it did not commend itself to all people. Now we come to the possibility that they had some justice on their side, apart from the forms which the clash took in this particular trial. We have noted that Socrates had derided poets and politicians; and to these the rhetoricians must be added, for despite the equivocal attitude taken toward rhetoric in the *Phaedrus,* Socrates rarely lost an opportunity for a sally against speechmakers. The result of his procedure was to make the dialectician appear to stand alone as the professor of wisdom and to exclude certain forms of cognition and expression which have a part in holding a culture together. It is not surprising that to the practitioners of these arts, his dialectic looked overgrown, even menacing. In truth it does require an extreme stand to rule out poetry, politics, and rhetoric. The use of a body of poetry in expressing the values of a culture will not be questioned except by one who takes the radical view presented by Plato in Book III of the *Republic.* But Socrates says in an early part of the *Apology* that when he went to the poets, he was ashamed to find that there was hardly a man present "who could not speak better than they about the poems they themselves had composed." But speak how? Poets are often lamentably poor dialecticians if you drag them away from their poetry and force them to use explicit discourse; however, if they are good poets, they show reasoning power enough for their poetry and contribute something to the mind of which dialectic is incapable: feeling and motion.

The art of politics, although it often repels us in its degraded forms, cannot be totally abandoned in favor of pure speculation. Politics is a practical art. As such, it is concerned with man as a spatiotemporal creature; hence some political activity must take the form of compromise and adjustment. There is a certain relativism in it as a process, which fact is entailed by the *conditio humana.* But dialectic itself can stray too far from the human condition, as Pericles no doubt could have told him. We need not question that Socrates was an incomparably better man than most of the politicians who ruled Athens. He makes the point himself, however, that had he entered public life, he would have been proceeded against much earlier. That may well have been true, yet one can hardly conclude from its likelihood that human society can do without political leadership. It may be granted too that the men of Athens needed to learn from his dialectic; still they could not have depended upon it exclusively. The trend of Socrates' remarks, here and elsewhere, is that dialectic is sufficient for all the needs of man.

The fact that Socrates had excited the rhetoricians against him is a point of special significance for our argument. We have noted that he liked to indulge in raillery against speechmakers. Now it is one thing to attack those who make verbal jugglery their stock-in-trade, but it is another to attack rhetoric as an art. This is the matter over which the *Phaedrus* arrives at its point of hesitation: Can rhetoric be saved by being divorced from those methods and techniques which are merely seductive? The answer which is given in the *Phaedrus* can be regarded as ambiguous. At the end of the dialogue the rhetorician seems to wind up, by the force of the argument, a dialectician. But no reader can be unaware that Plato has made extensive use of his great rhetorical skill to buttress his case, to help it over certain places, and to make it more persuasive. His instinct in practice told him that rhetoric must supply something that dialectic lacks. This calls for looking further at the nature of rhetoric.

Rhetoric is designed to move men's feelings in the direction of a goal. As such, it is concerned not with abstract individuals, but with men in being. Moreover, these men in being it has to consider in relation to forces in being. Rhetoric begins with the assumption that man is born into history. If he is to be moved, the arguments addressed to him must have historicity as well as logicality. To explain: when Aristotle opens his discussion of rhetoric in the celebrated treatise of that name, he asserts that it is a counterpart of dialectic. The two are distinguished by the fact that dialectic always tries to discover the real syllogism in the argument whereas rhetoric tries to discover the real means of persuasion. From this emerges a difference of procedure, in which dialectic makes use of inductions and syllogisms, whereas rhetoric makes use of examples and enthymemes. In fact, Aristotle explicitly calls the use of example "rhetorical induction," and he calls the enthymeme the "rhetorical syllogism." This bears out our idea that rhetoric must be concerned with real or historical situations, although dialectic can attain its goal in a self-existing realm of discourse. Now the example is something taken from life, and the force of the example comes from the fact that it *is* or *was*. It is the thing already possessed in experience and so it is the property of everyone through the sharing of a common past. Through examples, the rhetorician appeals to matters that everybody has in a sense participated in. These are the possible already made the actual, and the audience is expected to be moved by their historicity.

The relation of rhetoric to "things-in-being" appears even more closely in the "rhetorical syllogism." The enthymeme, as students of logic learn, is a syllogism with one of the propositions missing. The reason the missing proposition is omitted is that it is presumed to exist already in the mind of the one to whom the argument is addressed. The rhetorician simply recognizes the wide acceptance of this proposition and assumes it as part of his argument. Propositions which can be assumed in this manner are settled beliefs, standing convictions, and attitudes of the people.

They are the "topics" to which he goes for his sources of persuasion.

Through employment of the enthymeme, the rhetorician enters into a solidarity with the audience by tacitly agreeing with one of its perceptions of reality. This step of course enables him to pass on to his conclusion. If the rhetorician should say, "The magistrate is an elected official and must therefore heed the will of the people," he would be assuming a major premise, which is that "all elected officials must heed the will of the people." That unsupplied, yet conceded proposition, gives him a means by which he can obtain force for his argument. Therefore, quite as in the case of the example, he is resorting to something already acknowledged as "actual."

Aristotle continues his discussion of the two methods by pointing out that some persons cannot be reached by mere instruction. By the term "instruction" he signifies something of the order of logical demonstration. "Further, in dealing with certain persons, even if we possessed the most accurate scientific knowledge, we should not find it easy to persuade them by such knowledge. For scientific discourse is concerned with instruction, but in the case of such persons instruction is impossible; our proofs and arguments must rest on generally accepted principles, as we said in the *Topics*, when speaking of converse with the multitude."[4]

This also puts dialectic in a separate, though adjunct, realm. The mere demonstration of logical connections is not enough to persuade the commonalty, who instead have to be approached through certain "places" or common perceptions of reality. It is these, as we have now seen, which rhetoric assumes in its enthymemes, taking the ordi-

---

[4] Aristotle, *Rhetoric*, translated by Lane Cooper (London, 1932), 1355a.

nary man's understanding of things and working from that to something that needs to be made evident and compulsive. As for dialectic, if the motive for it is bad, it becomes sophistry; if it is good, it becomes a scientific demonstration, which may lie behind the rhetorical argument, but which is not equivalent to it.

In sum, dialectic is epistemological and logical; it is concerned with discriminating into categories and knowing definitions. While this has the indispensable function of promoting understanding in the realm of thought, by its very nature it does not tell man what he must do. It tells him how the terms and propositions which he uses are related. It permits him to use the name of a species as a term without ever attending to whether the species exists and therefore is a force in being. That would be sufficient if the whole destiny of man were to know. But we are reminded that the end of living is activity and not mere cognition. Dialectic, though being rational and intellectual, simply does not heed the imperatives of living, which help give direction to the thought of the man of wisdom. The individual who makes his approach to life through dialectic alone does violence to life through his abstractive process. At the same time he makes himself antisocial because his discriminations are apart from the organic feeling of the community for what goes on. By this analysis the dialectician is only half a wise man and hence something less than a philosopher king, inasmuch as he leaves out the urgent reality of the actual, with which all rulers and judges know they have to deal.

The conclusion of this is that a society cannot live without rhetoric. There are some things in which the group needs to believe which cannot be demonstrated to everyone rationally. Their acceptance is pressed upon us by a kind of moral imperative arising from the group as a whole. To put them to the test of dialectic alone is to destroy the basis of belief in them and to weaken the cohesiveness of society. Such beliefs always come to us couched in rhetorical terms, which tell us what attitudes to take. The crucial defect of dialectic alone is that it ends in what might be called social agnosticism. The dialectician knows, but he knows in a vacuum; or, he knows, but he is without knowledge of how to act. Unless he is sustained by faith at one end or the other—unless he embraced something before he began the dialectical process or unless he embraces it afterward—he remains an unassimilable social agnostic. Society does not know what to do with him because his very existence is a kind of satire or aspersion upon its necessity to act. Or, it does know what to do with him, in a very crude and unpleasant form: it will put him away. Those who have to cope with passing reality feel that neutrality is a kind of desertion. In addition to understanding, they expect a rhetoric of action, and we must concede them some claim to this.

In thus trying to isolate the pure dialectician, we have momentarily lost sight of Socrates. We recall, of course, that he did not in all of his acts evince this determination to separate himself from the life of his culture. He served the state loyally as a soldier, and he refused opportunity to escape after the state had condemned him. His reasoning, in some of its lines, supports the kind of identification with history which I am describing as that of the whole man. There is one telltale fact near the very end of his career which gives interesting if indirect confirmation that Socrates had his own doubts about the omnicompetence of dialectic. When Phaedo and his friends visited Socrates in the prison, they found him composing verses. A dream had told him to "make music and work at it." Previously he had supposed that philosophy was the highest kind of music, but now, near the time of his execution, being visited by the dream again, he obeyed literally by composing a hymn to the god whose festival had just been celebrated and by turning some stories of Aesop into verse. Perhaps this was a way of acknowledging that a part of his nature—the poetical, rhetorical part—had been too neglected as a result of his devotion to dialectic and of making a kind of atonement at the end.

Still, the indictment "too much of a dialectician" has not been quashed. The trial itself can be viewed as a supremely dramatic incident in a far longer and broader struggle between rationalism on the one hand and poetry and rhetoric (and belief) on the other. This conflict reappears in the later battle, between Hellenic philosophy with its strong rational bias and Christianity, which ended after centuries in sweeping victory for the latter. Christianity provided all that Greek dialectic left out. It spoke to the feelings, and what seems of paramount significance, it had its inception in an historical fact. The Christian always had the story of Jesus with which to start his homilies. He could argue from a fact, or at least what was accepted as one, and this at once put him on grounds to persuade. We may recall here Aristotle's observation that in conversing with the multitude you do not aim at fresh scientific instruction; you rest your arguments upon generally accepted principles and beliefs, or broadly speaking, on things received. Practically, the victory of Christianity over Hellenic rationalism bears out the soundness of this insight. The Christians have worked through the poetry of their great allegory and through appeal to many facts as having happened, for example, the lives of the saints. Dialectic has been present, because it is never absent from rational discourse, but rhetoric and poetry were there to make up the winning combination.

Hellenic rationalism waned before man's need for some kind of faith and before a pessimism about human nature which seems to develop as history lengthens. We have emphasized that dialectic leads toward an agnosticism of action. Even Socrates was constantly saying, "The one thing that I know is that I know nothing." The fiercely positive Hebrew and Christian faiths contain nothing of this. As for the darker side of man's nature, what can set this forth but a powerful rhetoric? Dialectic may prove it in a conditional way, but it is up to the elaboration and iteration of rhetoric to make it real and overwhelming. Dialectic alone leads to an unwarranted confidence, and this evidently is the reason that Nietzsche refers to Socrates as an "optimist." If there is one thing which the great preachers of Christianity have inculcated, it is the proneness of man to fall.[5] Without extensive use of the art of rhetoric, they would have been unable to accomplish this. The triumph and continuance of Christianity and Christian culture attest the power of rhetoric in holding men together and maintaining institutions. It is generally admitted that there is a strong element of Platonism in Christianity. But if Plato provided the reasoning, Paul and Augustine supplied the persuasion. What emerged from this could not be withstood even by the power of Rome.

One cannot doubt that the decay of this great support of Western culture is closely connected with the decline of rhetoric. I spoke earlier of a growing resentment against the orator. This resentment arises from a feeling, perhaps not

---

[5] This is also the point of the great tragedies written before Euripides, who, significantly, was the only tragedian that Socrates admired.

consciously articulated in many who possess it, that the orator is a teacher and a moral teacher at that. He cannot avoid being this if he uses words which will move men in a direction which he has chosen. But here is where the chief point of theoretical contention arises. There are persons today, some of them holding high positions in education, who believe (in theory, of course) that it is improper for any person to try to persuade another person. A name which has been invented for this act of persuading is "psychological coercion," which is obviously itself a highly loaded rhetorical phrase. From some such notion have come the extraordinary doctrines of modern semantics. According to the followers of this movement, the duty of anyone using language is to express the "facts" and avoid studiously the use of emotional coloring. The very use of facts in this kind of context reveals an astonishing naïveté about the nature of language. Yet there can be no doubt that this doctrine carries a great danger in that it represents a new attempt of dialectic to discredit and displace rhetoric. The writings of this group contain such a curious mélange of positivist dogma, modern prejudice, and liberal clichés that one runs a risk even in trying to digest it for purposes of analysis. Nevertheless, there are reasons for believing that it is in essence a new threat to fractionate society by enthroning dialectic as the only legitimate language of discourse.

The advocates of the "semantic" approach try to ascertain definitely the relationship between words and the things they stand for with the object of making signification more "scientific." These semanticists believe generally that traditional speech is filled with terms which stand for nonexistent things, empty ideas, and primitive beliefs which get in the way of man's adaptation to environment.

For them the function of speech is communication, and communication should be about things that really are. (One cannot read their literature very long without sensing the strong political motivation that inspires their position. A considerable part of their writing is a more or less open polemic against those features of speech which they regard as reflecting or upholding our traditional form of society. At a level below this, but for the same reason, they are antimetaphysical.) Unless we can establish that the world we are talking about is the world that exists empirically, then, the semanticists feel, we had better not talk at all. They want a vocabulary that is purified of all terms that originate in the subjectivity of the user, or at least they want to identify all such terms and place them in a quarantine ward.

The attempt must be identified as a fresh eruption of pure dialectic because it is concerned primarily with defining. Just as Socrates tried to define "justice" or "love" by now widening, now narrowing the categories, so they try, in a supposedly scientific way, to make the term fit the thing. The two are not engaged in exactly the same quest, and I shall come to their difference later, but they are both relying exclusively upon accurate verbal identification of something that is by them considered objective. As Socrates searched for the pure idea, so they search for the expression of the pure thing or fact. Moreover, they regard this as having the same power of salvation as the archetypal idea.

The quest of semantics cannot succeed, because the very theory of it is fallacious. The connection between a word and what it stands for cannot be determined in the way that they seem to believe. They operate on the assumption that there is some extralinguistic way of deciding what a word should mean, some point outside language from which one can judge the appropriateness of any choice of words for expression. The effort to get around language and to apply extralinguistic yardsticks is doomed to failure even in the cases of words symbolizing physical objects. A word stands for these things, but does not stand for them in the shape of the things. Language is a closed system, into which there is only one mode of entrance, and that is through meaning. And what a word means is going to be determined by the whole context of the vocabulary, with all the intermodification that this involves. A word does not get in through its fidelity to an object, but through its capacity to render what that object means to us.

But they do not even discriminate rightly the kinds of things for which words must stand. They assume that all words must stand for phenomena or things which are observable and classifiable by science. Indeed, this is their first principle: if a thing cannot be proved to exist scientifically —if it cannot be classified *with* phenomena—we are not supposed to bring it into expression at all, except in those relaxed moments when we are telling fairy stories and the like. Obviously they are ignoring the immensely important role of the subjective in life. There are numberless ideas, images, feelings, and intuitions which cannot be described and classified in the way of scientific phenomena but which have great effect upon our decisions. A rhetoric can take these into account, modify, direct, and use them because rhetoric deals in depth and tendency. A dialectic in the form of semantics cannot do this because it is interested only in defining words on the assumption that definitions are determined by the physical order. Just as the physical scientist discovers a law or a regularity in nature, so they endeavor to locate the source of terms in physical reality, and indeed their prime concern is to decide whether a referent really "exists." On first thought this might seem to give them the kind of respect for the actual order that I have claimed for believers in history. But a distinction is necessary: history is not the simple data of the perceptive consciousness; it is the experience of man after this has been assimilated and worked upon by the spirit. The appeal to history is an appeal to events made meaningful, and the meaning of events cannot be conveyed through the simple empirical references that semantic analysis puts forward as an ideal. Hence it is that the semanticist too is a neutralist, who would say, "Here is the world expressed in language that has been freed from tendency and subjective coloration." What is to be done with this world is postponed until another meeting, as it were, or it is assigned to a different kind of activity. His great mistake is the failure to see that language is intended to be sermonic. Because of its nature and of its intimacy with our feelings, it is always preaching. This type of agnostic will not listen to the sermon because he is unwilling to credit the existence of values. Yet even after it has been decided that the referent does exist, there is nothing to do with the word except turn it over to others whose horizons are not bounded by logical positivism.

This brings us to the necessity of concluding that the upholders of mere dialectic, whether they appear in this modern form or in another, are among the most subversive enemies of society and culture. They are attacking an ultimate source of cohesion in the interest of a doctrine which can issue only in nullity. It is of no service to man to impugn his feeling about the world qua feeling. Feeling is the source of that healthful tension between man and what *is*—both objectively and subjectively. If man could be brought to believe that all feeling about the world is wrong, there would be nothing for him but collapse.

Socrates was saved from trivialization of their kind by his initial commitment to the Beautiful and the Good. He is also saved in our eyes by the marvelous rhetoric of Plato. These were not enough to save him personally in the great crisis of his life, but they give high seriousness to the quest which he represents. The modern exponents of dialectic have nothing like these to give respectability to their undertaking or persuasiveness to their cause. But both, in the long view, are the victims of supposing that definition and classification are sufficient as the ends of speech.

In a summing up we can see that dialectic, when not accompanied by a historical consciousness and responsibility, works to dissolve those opinions, based partly on feeling, which hold a society together. It tends, therefore, to be essentially revolutionary and without commitment to practical realities. It is even contumacious toward the "given," ignoring it or seeking to banish it in favor of a merely self-consistent exposition of ideas.

Rhetoric, on the other hand, tries to bring opinion into closer line with the truth which dialectic pursues. It is therefore cognizant of the facts of situations and it is at least understanding of popular attitudes.

There is a school of thinking, greatly influenced by the Socratic tradition, which holds that it is intellectually treasonable to take popular opinion into account. The side that one espouses in this issue will be determined by his attitude toward creation. When we look upon the "given" of the world, we find two things: the world itself and the opinions which mankind has about the world. Both of these must be seen as parts of the totality. The world is a primary creation, and the opinions of men are creations of the men who live in it. Next the question becomes: can we regard the world as infinitely correctable and men's opinions of it as of no account? Socrates could do this because he believed in a god or gods. The world is by him from the beginning condemned; it is a prison house, a dark cave; it is the realm of becoming which is destined to pass away. All things tend toward realizing themselves in a godlikeness, at which time the mortal and earthly will have been shuffled off. A complete reliance upon dialectic becomes possible only if one accepts something like this Socratic theodicy. But the important point is that it denies the axiological status of creation.

The modern counterpart thinks he can affirm that creation is infinitely correctable because he believes only in man and speaks only on his behalf. When we examine his position, however, we find that he believes only in the natural order. This he reveals by his insistence upon positivistic proof for everything. But from the positive order he cannot draw the right inferences about man. He can find no place for those creations like affections and opinions which are distinctly human and which are part of the settlement of any culture. For him an opinion, instead of being a stage of historical consciousness which may reflect a perfectly bona fide if narrow experience, is just an impediment in the way of the facts. His dialectic would move toward the facts and seek to destroy that which holds the facts in a cohesive picture. On his principle a cohesive or systematized outlook must involve distortion, and this explains why he automatically refers to rhetoric as "propaganda."

In brief the dialectician of our day has no adequate theory of man. Lacking such a theory, he of course cannot find a place for rhetoric, which is the most humanistic of all the disciplines. Rhetoric speaks to man in his whole being and out of his whole past and with reference to values which only a human being can intuit. The semanticists have in view only a denatured speech to suit a denatured man. Theirs is a major intellectual error, committed by supposing that they were going to help man by bringing language under the surveillance of science.

There is never any question that rhetoric ultimately will survive this scientistic attack. The pity is that the attacks should ever have been made at all since, proceeding from contempt for history and ignorance of the nature of man, they must produce confusion, skepticism, and inaction. In the restored man dialectic and rhetoric will go along hand in hand as the regime of the human faculties intended that they should do. That is why the recovery of value and of community in our time calls for a restatement of the broadly cultural role of rhetoric.

Some people believe it is improper for one per-
son to try to influence another. . . . "Don't med-
dle with their opinions, but teach them to think
and form their own" is the basis of this school of
thought. . . . This dialectic ends up in social
agnosticism.

—RICHARD M. WEAVER, unpublished lecture
delivered at the University of Arkansas
November 8, 1961

The teacher is, according to Weaver, a "definer," a "namer," and an "orderer" of the universe of meanings. After all, he argues, the "world has to be named for the benefit of each oncoming generation." Those who give the names have a unique role in ordering and controlling society.

This essay is a plea for teachers of speech, language, and composition—who are the primary orderers—to "teach the truth" by "teaching names which are indexes to essences." Nowhere in Weaver's writings is his conception of ultimate reality more clearly stated than in "To Write the Truth."

To Write the Truth

THE ENDLESS effort toward refurbishing college composition, with its restless shift of approach, of sequence, of emphasis, arouses suspicion that the most formidable question of all has been begged. A course so firmly intrenched in every curriculum and yet so productive of dissatisfaction must conceal a problem which needs to be set forth in its true nature and proportion.

For this reason I wish to make a certain radical, and probably impolitic, inquiry about objectives. Suppose it were possible to poll every teacher of college composition with reference to its aims; is it likely that any area of unanimous agreement could be found? I am aware of the varied philosophies, but if the question is properly phrased, my surmise is Yes; I cannot imagine anyone's denying that the aim of a course in composition is to make students more articulate. Every instructor wishes his students to write better, to talk better, and is chagrined if tests cast doubt upon the achievement. He may steal moments to introduce them to the sweetness and light of literature, but

his success is measured by how his charges gain facility with
their native tongue. That, at least, is the plain implication
of syllabuses, course plans, and examinations. I suspect,
however, that just here lies the root of our commonly felt
frustration; we are not conceiving the real nature of our
duty if we stop with making students articulate, even to the
point of eloquence.

For at the source of our feeling of restlessness and incomplete achievement is the ignoring of a question necessarily
prior: About what do we wish to make men articulate?
Admittedly we who instruct in the art of speech are turning
loose upon the world a power. Where do we expect the
wielders of that power to learn the proper use of it? Now
"proper" is, of course, a critical word, and I propose next to
examine its possible meanings.

There came a moment in the fourteenth century when
teachers of rhetoric and philosophy hesitated between two
aims: Was it their duty to teach men *vere loqui* or *recte
loqui*, in the phrases then employed? Obviously a basic
question of epistemology was involved. Those who favored
the former were metaphysicians; those who favored the
latter had come to believe, as Bacon expressed it in the
Advancement of Learning, that "the Essential Forms or
true differences of things cannot by any human diligence be
found out." Empiricism was gathering strength, and the
decision was to teach *recte loqui*, as one can discover in the
manuals of rhetoric of the Renaissance. Once the ontological referents were given up, however, this proved but an
intermediate stage, and the course continued until today
we can discern on all sides a third aim, which I shall take
the liberty of phrasing in a parallel way as *utiliter loqui*.
From speaking truthfully to speaking correctly to speaking

usefully—is this not the rhetorician's easy descent to Avernus?

Yet these changes seem to be symptomatic of a profound trend, and it is to be feared that the course of our civilization is mirrored in the direction they indicate. The teacher of composition today, who thinks he is struggling merely with the ignorance and indifferentism of individuals, is actually trying to hold back the tide which is threatening intellectual life as such. Perhaps the picture seems melodramatic. I think it will seem less so after we have examined the implications of the trend.

Let us begin with our own time and look at *utiliter loqui*, which is usually described as a potent handmaiden of Success. It is the art of using language to better our position in the world—and heaven knows its objective comports with a great deal that has been said from high places about the aim of education. That knowledge is power has been dinned at us until it appears faintly treasonable to question the pragmatic use of speech. But, in all candor, is it the goal of our instruction in expression, both written and oral, to make men more eloquent about their passions and their interests? It would hardly do to reason from actual practice, for a large part of the teaching of composition facilitates and perhaps encourages such proficiency. From it comes the language of journalism and advertising; from it comes the language of those who study rhetoric with the object of making the worse appear the better cause. In technical and professional schools the aim may be frankly indicated in catalogue descriptions; language is a tool which will enable you to get what you want if you use it well—and well does not mean scrupulously. Says George F. Babbitt to his son Ted, who is having his evening struggle with *Comus* and Cicero, "Be a good bit better if you took Business English, and learned how to write an ad, or a letter that would pull." Millions will agree on the point with Babbitt, and plenty have paid hard cash for training which they were told would enable them to place eloquence in the service of popularity or profit.

Those who teach English on this level are the modern sophists, as the homely realism of the world seems to recognize. They are doing what the orators were once accused of doing, making speech the harlot of the arts. More specifically, they are using the element of universality in language for purposes which actually set men against one another. They are teaching their students how to prevail with what is, finally, verbal deception.

Now *recte loqui,* because it teaches a sort of etiquette, appears more respectable; and therein lies its danger. It is the way of those who wish their speech to bear the stamp of conventional correctness. They have their eyes, therefore, upon tradition, or upon the practice of a dominant class, since they desire their style of utterance to indicate that they belong. They are more fearful of a misplaced accent than of an ambiguity, because the former arouses suspicion that they have not been with the right people. This is the language favored by the timid, who live in fear of conventions, and by the ambitious, who have learned how to use conventions as a means of self-promotion. Making allowance for those who see an ideal in purism, we can yet say that this is speech which is socially useful, and thus we are not in much better plight if we confine ourselves circumspectly to the teaching of *recte loqui.* The acceptance of such assignment still leaves the teacher indifferent to truth. He has no standard other than what was done, if he is a traditionalist, or what is being done, if he is a pragmatist. A large body of opinion, of course, believes that this is precisely the teacher's job; he is paid to be an interpreter and an upholder of established institutions; he initiates the young into the mysteries but does not question them himself. Every teacher has to make this choice between play actor and prophet, and most of them choose the play actor. The public must suspect this hopelessly servile role when it snickers at caricatures of teachers.

Certainly nothing creative and nothing revolutionary (which in the best sense is creative) can come from this dancing of attendance upon fashion in speech. It means in the nature of things a limitation to surfaces; indeed, it leaves one without a real standard of what is right, for the most massive traditions undergo change, and the teacher may at any moment find himself faced with competing old and new ways and without a criterion to judge between them. In sum, *recte loqui* requires the language of social property. Because it reflects more than anything else a worldliness or satisfaction with existing institutions, it is the speech of pragmatic acquiescence. Whoso stops here confesses that education is only instruction in mores. Is it any wonder that professors have been contemptuously grouped with dancing masters, sleight-of-hand artists, and vendors of patent medicine?

If now we are not resigned to the teaching of sophistry or of etiquette, there remains only the severe and lofty discipline of *vere loqui*. This means teaching people to speak the truth, which can be done only by giving them the right names of things. We approach here a critical point in the argument, which will determine the possibility of defining what is correct in expression; we come in fact to the relationship of sign and thing signified.

Since this involves the inherent rightness of names, let us

consider for a moment the child's statement: "Pigs are called 'pigs' because they are filthy beasts." The semanticists offer this as an outstanding example of fatuity, but what, I would ask, are the alternatives? They are: "Pigs are called 'pigs' because that is what they have been called for a long time," and "Pigs are called 'pigs' because this name gives one a degree of control, as when summoning them to the trough." After all, there is something to be said for the child's interpretation. It presents an attachment of thing and concept. The others, in accepting tradition and in seeking utility, offer reasoning which is merely circular. The first says that what is, is; and the second affirms in good pragmatic vein that what works, works. I would not argue that the child has the whole philosophy of the matter; but he appears to be seeking the road to understanding; he is trying to get at the nature of the thing, and such must be the endeavor of all who seek a bridge to the real.

Now every teacher is for his students an Adam. They come to him trusting in his power to bestow the right names on things. "And out of the ground the Lord God formed every beast of the field, and every fowl of the air, and brought them unto Adam to see what he would call them; and whatever Adam called every living creature, that was the name thereof." The naming of the beasts and the fowls was one of the most important steps in creation. Adam helped to order the universe when he dealt out these names, and let us not overlook what is implied in the assertion that the names stuck. There is the intimation of divine approval, which would frown upon capricious change. A name is not just an accident; neither is it a convention which can be repealed by majority vote at the next meeting; once a thing has been given a name, it appears to have a certain autonomous right to that name, so that it could not be changed without imperiling the foundations of the world.

If I begin to seem fanciful here, let us recall that Plato was deeply interested in this problem, as one can discover by reading the *Cratylus*. And he could accept the view neither that a name is an accident nor that it is a convention which a man or a state may alter at will. For him—and we should wonder why teachers have not pondered this more—a name is "a means of *teaching* and of separating reality." The word in the original is *didaskalikon*. Consequently, he goes on to add, a teacher is one who gives names well, and "well means like a teacher." Because those who give the names are in a unique position to control, the task is not to be intrusted to just anyone. "Then it is not for everyman, Hermogenes," he makes Socrates declare, "to give names, but for him who may be called the namemaker; and he, it appears, is the lawgiver, who is of all artisans among men the rarest." Plato then proceeds to a conclusion that since the namemaker is the lawgiver, he must, if he is to make proper use of this *organon didaskalikon*, have a dialectician sitting by his side. By thus arranging a philosophical supervision for name-giving, he establishes his point that name-giving is not a task for "trifling and casual persons." Certainly no one blind to the unities and pluralities of the world can be placed in charge of what things are to be called.

The task now begins to appear serious indeed, for those engaged in separating reality are in effect ordering the universe. The burden of some teachers is in fact heavier than Adam's, for teaching the names of imponderables is far more difficult and dangerous than teaching those of animals and rocks. The world has to be named for the benefit of each oncoming generation, and who teaches more names than the arbiter of the use of language? With the primer one begins to call the roll of things, and the college essay is but an extended definition.

Suppose a teacher, striving to vitalize his instruction, as the professors of education like to put it, assigns his papers on current topics. What is he to tell students, by way of preparation or correction, that "democracy" is the name of? Does it stand for something existing in the nature of things, something in accordance with "right reason," or can it be changed overnight to mean dictatorship of the proletariat? And what of "freedom"? Does it stand for an area in which the individual is sovereign, or does it signify some wide function of a centralized government? What sense of direction is carried by the term "progressive"? Consider the immeasurable harm one might do students by telling them that "history" is the name of our recollection of the past adjusted to suit our feelings and aspirations, as some recent historians would have us do.

I am not unaware of the questions which will come crowding in at this point. It will be asked: By what act of arrogance do we imagine that we know what things really are? The answer to this is: By what act of arrogance do we set ourselves up as teachers? There are two postulates basic to our profession: the first is that one man can know more than another, and the second is that such knowledge can be imparted. Whoever cannot accept both should retire from the profession and renounce the intention of teaching anyone anything.

Let those who consider such prerogative unreasonable consider what remains. If we cannot be sure that one person knows better than another the true nature of things, then we should follow the logic of our convictions and choose our teachers as the ancient Greek democracies chose their magistrates, by lot. Let us imagine that on some appointed November day we here in Chicago proceed to Soldiers Field, and there from a huge kettle we draw lots, and those drawing, say, the blue slips become automatically the school staff for the ensuing year. This mode of selection would surely be mandatory under the proposition that one man knows as much truth as another about the things that are to be passed on to the next generation. I do not think the scheme would meet with popular approval. In fact, I suspect that it would be denounced as radical. We should have to go back then and say that whoever is willing to make the most elementary predication acknowledges thereby that he thinks he has some grasp upon reality, which is a form of saying that he thinks he possesses some measure of the truth. Such people only may be certificated to teach. For those who doubt the existence of truth, there is only what Santayana has called "the unanswerable scepticism of silence."

There is no escape from this in the plea that, since there are today many competing ideologies, it is usurpation for the teacher to make his own the standard. Such policy throws us right into the embrace of relativism, which leaves us as helpless as the skepticism outlined above. It is very hard after a century of liberalism, with its necessity of avoiding commitment, to get people to admit the possibility of objective truth, but here again we are face to face with our dilemma: if it does not exist, there is nothing to teach; if it does exist, how can we conceive of allowing anyone to teach anything else? Those who argue that teachers should confine themselves to presenting all sides of every question—in our instance, to giving all the names previously and currently applied to a thing—are tacitly assuming that there are sources closer to the truth than are the schools and that the schools merely act as their agents. It would be interesting to hear what these sources are.

Here is the point at which teachers have to make up their minds as to whether they are the "trifling and casual" persons described by Plato. Either they are going to teach sophistry and etiquette, or they are going to teach names which are indexes to essences. I will grant that the latter course makes teachers of composition philosophers more truly than those who teach the systems of philosophy, but there is no alternative short of that disastrous abdication which says, "Write anything you please as long as you write it well." This is invocation to the asocial muse. Just anything the uninstructed mind pleases cannot be written well. Even on the most practical level there is no such separation between substance and form of utterance. Anyone who has observed the teaching of composition knows that, regardless of how much latitude of sentiment the instructor gives himself credit for, there will be judgment of idea. When the comment is made that a paper "says something," it is being valued for recognizing a measure of reality or for being true in its assertions. Ultimately there is no evading the issue of whether any piece of writing predicates something about the world, either literally or imaginatively, and this is why I am arguing that, in teaching students to be articulate, we must hold up the standard of what is true. The man who essays that task is doctor of philosophy in more than title, and he takes on stature.

Perhaps I should visualize for a moment the course I am urging. Here is our teacher, who is charged with the awful responsibility of telling a younger generation the true names of things, figuratively sitting with the dialectician at his elbow. What is the use of this counselor? I should say that his chief function is to keep the teacher out of the excluded middle. He is able to define, and he can see contradictions, and he is never going to say that B is only a mode of A. In short, he is going to stand guard against that relativism which has played havoc with so many things and which is now attacking language. He will save those points of reference which are disappearing as we fall into the trap of "infinite-valued orientation." The dialectician works through logic, which is itself an assurance that the world has order. True enough, there will not be much student-centered education here, and knowledge will take on an authority which some mistake for arrogance. The student will learn, however, that the world is not wholly contingent, but partly predictable, and that, if he will use his mind rightly, it will not lie to him about the world.

Let there be no mistake; this is an invitation to lead the dangerous life. Whoso comes to define comes bearing the sword of division. The teacher will find himself not excluded from the world but related to it in ways that may become trying. But he will regain something that has been lost in the long dilution of education, the standing of one with a mission. He will be able, as he has not been for a long while, to take his pay partly in honor.

It is often thoughtlessly said that the restoration of our broken world lies largely in the hands of the teachers. The statement is true, but the implications are not drawn. The teachers cannot contribute by teaching more disorder. When something has been broken, the repairman fixes it, with his mind not on the broken object but on the form according to which it was originally made. And so we who must repair some names that have fallen into strange distortions must not consult the distorted shapes but rather conceive the archetypes for which they stood.

A prominent educator was recently heard to declare that

he hoped for a day when people would point with admiration to a member of the teaching profession and say, "Look, he is a teacher." We may be sure that day will not dawn until the remark carries the implication, "Look, he is a definer." For this reason teachers who think they have a part in the redemption of society will have to desert certain primrose paths of dalliance and begin the difficult, the dangerous, work of teaching men to speak and to write the truth.

I remember your question about the phrase "Language is Sermonic." The University of Oklahoma has invited me to give a short seminar in rhetoric at an advanced level this coming summer. One of the duties will be to give a formal lecture, and I have about decided that the subject shall be "Language is Sermonic." It is as yet not only unwritten but unthought-out; when I do get to work on it, though, I may be after you for some help.

—RICHARD M. WEAVER TO RALPH T. EUBANKS
November 14, 1961

I did conduct the seminar in rhetoric at Oklahoma for one week during a torrid July. The lecture "Language Is Sermonic" was delivered, though before a small audience.

—RICHARD M. WEAVER TO RALPH T. EUBANKS
November 17, 1962

The phrase "Language Is Sermonic" is a fitting capstone to Weaver's philosophy of rhetoric for, in his mind, "the rhetorician is a preacher to us, noble if he tries to direct our passion toward noble ends and base if he uses our passion to confuse and degrade us." Weaver thought we were all rhetoricians—"preachers in private or public capacities" who have "no sooner uttered words than we have given impulse to other people to look at the world . . . in our way."

In a sense "Language Is Sermonic" is the fullest and most mature statement of Richard M. Weaver as a rhetorical theorist. "The *Phaedrus* and the Nature of Rhetoric" establishes the philosophical base for his rhetorical theory, while "Language Is Sermonic" synthesizes his answers to the persistent questions arising from this philosophical base.

Language Is Sermonic

Our age has witnessed the decline of a number of subjects that once enjoyed prestige and general esteem, but no subject, I believe, has suffered more amazingly in this respect than rhetoric. When one recalls that a century ago rhetoric was regarded as the most important humanistic discipline taught in our colleges—when one recalls this fact and contrasts it with the very different situation prevailing today—he is forced to see that a great shift of valuation has taken place. In those days, in the not-so-distant Nineteenth Century, to be a professor of rhetoric, one had to be *somebody*. This was a teaching task that was thought to call for ample and varied resources, and it was recognized as addressing itself to the most important of all ends, the persuading of human beings to adopt right attitudes and act in response to them. That was no assignment for the plodding sort of professor. That sort of teacher might do a middling job with subject matter courses, where the main object is to impart information, but the teacher of rhetoric had to be a person of gifts and imagination who could illustrate, as the need arose, how to make words even in prose take on wings. I remind you of the chairs of rhetoric that still survive in title in some of our older universities. And I should add, to develop the full picture, that literature was then viewed as a subject which practically anyone could teach. No special gift, other than perhaps industry, was needed to relate facts about authors and periods. That was held to be rather pedestrian work. But the instructor in rhetoric was expected to be a man of stature. Today, I scarcely need point out, the situation has been exactly reversed. Today it is the teacher of literature who passes through a long period of training, who is supposed to possess the mysteries of a learned craft, and who is placed by his very speciality on a height of eminence. His knowledge of the intricacies of Shakespeare or Keats or Joyce and his sophistication in the critical doctrines that have been developed bring him the esteem of the academy. We must recognize in all fairness that the elaboration of critical techniques and special approaches has made the teaching of literature a somewhat more demanding profession, although some think that it has gone in that direction beyond the point of diminishing returns. Still, this is not enough to account for the relegation of rhetoric. The change has gone so far that now it is discouraging to survey the handling of this study in our colleges and universities. With a few honorable exceptions it is given to just about anybody who will take it. The "inferior, unlearned, mechanical, merely instrumental members of the profession" —to recall a phrase of a great master of rhetoric, Edmund Burke—have in their keeping what was once assigned to the leaders. Beginners, part-time teachers, graduate students, faculty wives, and various fringe people, are now the instructional staff of an art which was once supposed to require outstanding gifts and mature experience. (We must note that at the same time the course itself has been allowed to decline from one dealing philosophically with the problems of expression to one which tries to bring below-par students up to the level of accepted usage.) Indeed, the wheel of fortune would seem to have turned for rhetoric; what was once at the top is now at the bottom, and because of its low estate, people begin to wonder on what terms it can survive at all.

We are not faced here, however, with the wheel of fortune; we are faced with something that has come over the minds of men. Changes that come over the minds of men are not inscrutable, but have at some point their identifiable causes. In this case we have to deal with the most potent of cultural causes, an alteration of man's image of man. Something has happened in the recent past to our concept of what man is; a decision was made to look upon him in a new light, and from this decision new bases of evaluation have proceeded, which affect the public reputation of rhetoric. This changed concept of man is best described by the word "scientistic," a term which denotes the application of scientific assumptions to subjects which are not wholly comprised of naturalistic phenomena. Much of this is a familiar tale, but to understand the effect of the change, we need to recall that the great success of scientific or positivistic thinking in the Nineteenth Century induced a belief that nothing was beyond the scope of its method. Science, and its off-spring applied science, were doing so much to alter and, it was thought, to improve the material conditions of the world, that a next step with the same process seemed in order. Why should not science turn its apparatus upon man, whom all the revelations of religion and the speculations of philosophy seemed still to have left an enigma, with the promise of much better result? It came to be believed increasingly that to think validly was to think scientifically, and that subject matters made no difference.

Now the method of scientific investigation is, as T. H. Huxley reminded us in a lecture which does great credit to him as a rhetorician, merely the method of logic. Induction and deduction and causal inference applied to the phenomena of nature yielded the results with which science was changing the landscape and revolutionizing the modes of industry. From this datum it was an easy inference that men ought increasingly to become scientists, and again, it was a simple derivative from this notion that man at his best is a logic machine, or at any rate an austerely unemotional thinker. Furthermore, carried in the train of this conception was the thought, not often expressed of course, that things would be better if men did not give in so far to being human in the humanistic sense. In the shadow of the victories of science, his humanism fell into progressive disparagement. Just what comprises humanism is not a simple matter for analysis. Rationality is an indispensable part to be sure, yet humanity includes emotionality, or the capacity to feel and suffer, to know pleasure, and it includes the capacity for aesthetic satisfaction, and, what can be only suggested, a yearning to be in relation with something infinite. This last is his religious passion, or his aspiration to feel significant and to have a sense of belonging in a world that is productive of much frustration. These at least are the properties of humanity. Well, man had been human for some thousands of years, and where had it gotten him? Those who looked forward to a scientific Utopia were inclined to think that his humanness had been a drag on his progress; human qualities were weaknesses, except for that special quality of rationality, which might be expected to redeem him.

However curious it may appear, this notion gained that man should live down his humanity and make himself a more efficient source of those logical inferences upon which a scientifically accurate understanding of the world depends. As the impulse spread, it was the emotional and subjective components of his being that chiefly came under criticism, for reasons that have just been indicated. Emotion and logic or science do not consort; the latter must be objective, faithful to what is out there in the public domain and conformable to the processes of reason. Whenever emotion is allowed to put in an oar, it gets the boat off true course. Therefore emotion is a liability.

Under the force of this narrow reasoning, it was natural that rhetoric should pass from a status in which it was regarded as of questionable worth to a still lower one in which it was positively condemned. For the most obvious truth about rhetoric is that its object is the whole man. It presents its arguments first to the rational part of man, because rhetorical discourses, if they are honestly conceived, always have a basis in reasoning. Logical argument is the plot, as it were, of any speech or composition that is designed to persuade. Yet it is the very characterizing feature of rhetoric that it goes beyond this and appeals to other parts of man's constitution, especially to his nature as a pathetic being, that is, a being feeling and suffering. A speech intended to persuade achieves little unless it takes into account how men are reacting subjectively to their hopes and fears and their special circumstances. The fact that Aristotle devotes a large proportion of his *Rhetoric* to how men feel about different situations and actions is an evidence of how prominently these considerations bulked even in the eyes of a master theorist.

Yet there is one further fact, more decisive than any of these, to prove that rhetoric is addressed to man in his humanity. Every speech which is designed to move is directed to a special audience in its unique situation. (We could not except even those radio appeals to "the world." Their audience has a unique place in time.) Here is but a way of pointing out that rhetoric is intended for historical man, or for man as conditioned by history. It is part of the *conditio humana* that we live at particular times and in particular places. These are productive of special or unique urgencies, which the speaker has got to recognize and to estimate. Hence, just as man from the point of view of rhetoric is not purely a thinking machine, or a mere seat of rationality, so he is not a creature abstracted from time and place. If science deals with the abstract and the universal, rhetoric is near the other end, dealing in significant part with the particular and the concrete. It would be the height of wishful thinking to say that this ought not be so. As long as man is born into history, he will be feeling and responding to historical pressures. All of these reasons combine to show why rhetoric should be considered the most humanistic of the humanities. It is directed to that part of our being which is not merely rational, for it supplements the rational approach. And it is directed to individual men in their individual situations, so that by the very definitions of the terms here involved, it takes into account what science deliberately, to satisfy its own purposes, leaves out. There is consequently no need for wonder that, in an age that has been influenced to distrust and disregard what is characteristically human, rhetoric should be a prime target of attack.

If it is a weakness to harbor feelings, and if furthermore it is a weakness to be caught up in historical situations, then rhetoric is construable as a dealer in weaknesses. That man is in this condition religion, philosophy, and literature have been teaching for thousands of years. Criticism of it from the standpoint of a scientistic Utopia is the new departure.

The incompleteness of the image of man as a creature who should make use of reason only can be demonstrated in another way. It is a truism that logic is a subject without a subject matter. That is to say, logic is a set of rules and devices which are equally applicable whatever the data. As the science of the forms of reasoning, it is a means of interpreting and utilizing the subject matters of the various fields which do have their proper contents. Facts from science or history or literature, for example, may serve in the establishment of an inductive generalization. Similar facts may be fed into a syllogism. Logic is merely the mechanism for organizing the data of other provinces of knowledge. Now it follows from this truth that if a man could convert himself into a pure logic machine or thinking machine, he would have no special relation to any body of knowledge. All would be grist for his mill, as the phrase goes. He would have no inclination, no partiality, no particular affection. His mind would work upon one thing as indifferently as upon another. He would be an eviscerated creature or a depassionated one, standing in the same relationship to the realities of the world as the thinking technique stands to the data on which it is employed. He would be a thinking robot, a concept which horrifies us precisely because the robot has nothing to think about.

A confirmation of this truth lies in the fact that rhetoric can never be reduced to symbology. Logic is increasingly becoming "symbolic logic"; that is its tendency. But rhetoric always comes to us in well-fleshed words, and that is because it must deal with the world, the thickness, stubbornness, and power of it.[1]

Everybody recognizes that there is thus a formal logic. A number of eminent authorities have written of rhetoric as if it were formal in the same sense and degree. Formal rhetoric would be a set of rules and devices for persuading anybody about anything. If one desires a certain response, one uses a certain device, or "trick" as the enemies of the art would put it. The set of appeals that rhetoric provides is analogized with the forms of thought that logic prescribes. Rhetoric conceived in this fashion has an adaptability and virtuosity equal to those of logic.

But the comparison overlooks something, for at one point we encounter a significant difference. Rhetoric has a relationship to the world which logic does not have and which forces the rhetorician to keep an eye upon reality as well as upon the character and situation of his audience. The truth of this is seen when we begin to examine the nature of the traditional "topics." The topics were first formulated by Aristotle and were later treated also by Cicero and Quintilian and by many subsequent writers on the subject of persuasion. They are a set of "places" or "regions" where one can go to find the substance for persuasive argument. Cicero defines a topic as "the seat of an argument." In function they are sources of content for speeches that are designed to influence. Aristotle listed a considerable number of them, but for our purposes they can be categorized very broadly. In reading or interpreting

[1] I might add that a number of years ago the Mathematics Staff of the College at the University of Chicago made a wager with the English Staff that they could write the Declaration of Independence in mathematical language. They must have had later and better thoughts about this, for we never saw the mathematical rendition.

the world of reality, we make use of four very general ideas. The first three are usually expressed, in the language of philosophy, as being, cause, and relationship. The fourth, which stands apart from these because it is an external source, is testimony and authority.

One way to interpret a subject is to define its nature—to describe the fixed features of its being. Definition is an attempt to capture essence. When we speak of the nature of a thing, we speak of something we expect to persist. Definitions accordingly deal with fundamental and unchanging properties.

Another way to interpret a subject is to place it in a cause-and-effect relationship. The process of interpretation is then to affirm it as the cause of some effect or as the effect of some cause. And the attitudes of those who are listening will be affected according to whether or not they agree with our cause-and-effect analysis.

A third way to interpret a subject is in terms of relationships of similarity and dissimilarity. We say that it is like something which we know in fuller detail, or that it is unlike that thing in important respects. From such a comparison conclusions regarding the subject itself can be drawn. This is a very common form of argument, by which probabilities can be established. And since probabilities are all we have to go on in many questions of this life, it must be accounted a usable means of persuasion.

The fourth category, the one removed from the others by the fact of its being an external source, deals not with the evidence directly but accepts it on the credit of testimony or authority. If we are not in position to see or examine, but can procure the deposition of some one who is, the deposition may become the substance of our argument. We can slip it into a syllogism just as we would a defined term. The same is true of general statements which come from quarters of great authority or prestige. If a proposition is backed by some weighty authority, like the Bible, or can be associated with a great name, people may be expected to respond to it in accordance with the veneration they have for these sources. In this way evidence coming from the outside is used to influence attitudes or conduct.

Now we see that in all these cases the listener is being asked not simply to follow a valid reasoning form but to respond to some presentation of reality. He is being asked to agree with the speaker's interpretation of the world that is. If the definition being offered is a true one, he is expected to recognize this and to say, at least inwardly, "Yes, that is the way the thing is." If the exposition of cause-and-effect relationship is true, he may be expected to concur that X is the cause of such a consequence or that such a consequence has its cause in X. And according to whether this is a good or a bad cause or a good or a bad consequence, he is disposed to preserve or remove the cause, and so on. If he is impressed with the similarity drawn between two things, he is as a result more likely to accept a policy which involves treating something in the same way in which its analogue is treated. He has been influenced by a relationship of comparability. And finally, if he has been confronted with testimony or authority from sources he respects, he will receive this as a reliable, if secondary, kind of information about reality. In these four ways he has been persuaded to read the world as the speaker reads it.

At this point, however, I must anticipate an objection. The retort might be made: "These are extremely formal categories you are enumerating. I fail to see how they are any less general or less indifferently applicable than the formal categories of logic. After all, definitions and so on can be offered of anything. You still have not succeeded in making rhetoric a substantive study."

In replying, I must turn here to what should be called the office of rhetoric. Rhetoric seen in the whole conspectus of its function is an art of emphasis embodying an order of desire. Rhetoric is advisory; it has the office of advising men with reference to an independent order of goods and with reference to their particular situation as it relates to these. The honest rhetorician therefore has two things in mind: a vision of how matters should go ideally and ethically and a consideration of the special circumstances of his auditors. Toward both of these he has a responsibility.

I shall take up first how his responsibility to the order of the goods or to the hierarchy of realities may determine his use of the topics.

When we think of rhetoric as one of the arts of civil society (and it must be a free society, since the scope for rhetoric is limited and the employment of it constrained under a despotism) we see that the rhetorician is faced with a choice of means in appealing to those whom he can prevail upon to listen to him. If he is at all philosophical, it must occur to him to ask whether there is a standard by which the sources of persuasion can be ranked. In a phrase, is there a preferred order of them, so that, in a scale of ethics, it is nobler to make use of one sort of appeal than another? This is of course a question independent of circumstantial matters, yet a fundamental one. We all react to some rhetoric as "untruthful" or "unfair" or "cheap," and this very feeling is evidence of the truth that it is possible to use a better or a worse style of appeal. What is the measure of the better style? Obviously this question cannot be answered at all in the absence of some conviction about the nature and destiny of man. Rhetoric inevita-

bly impinges upon morality and politics; and if it is one of
the means by which we endeavor to improve the character
and the lot of men, we have to think of its methods and
sources in relation to a scheme of values.

To focus the problem a little more sharply, when one is
asking men to cooperate with him in thinking this or doing
that, when is he asking in the name of the highest reality,
which is the same as saying, when is he asking in the name
of their highest good?

Naturally, when the speaker replies to this question, he is
going to express his philosophy, or more precisely, his metaphysics. My personal reply would be that he is making the
highest order of appeal when he is basing his case on
definition or the nature of the thing. I confess that this goes
back to a very primitive metaphysics, which holds that the
highest reality is being, not becoming. It is a quasi-religious
metaphysics, if you will, because it ascribes to the highest
reality qualities of stasis, immutability, eternal perdurance
—qualities that in Western civilization are usually expressed in the language of theism. That which is perfect
does not change; that which has to change is less perfect.
Therefore, if it is possible to determine unchanging essences or qualities and to speak in terms of these, one is
appealing to what is most real in so doing. From another
point of view, this is but getting people to see what is most
permanent in existence, or what transcends the world of
change and accident. The realm of essence is the realm
above the flux of phenomena, and definitions are of essences and genera.

I may have expressed this view in somewhat abstruse
language in order to place it philosophically, yet the practice I am referring to is everyday enough, as a simple
illustration will make plain. If a speaker should define man

as a creature with an indefeasible right to freedom and should upon this base an argument that a certain man or group of men are entitled to freedom, he would be arguing from definition. Freedom is an unchanging attribute of his subject; it can accordingly be predicated of whatever falls within the genus man. Stipulative definitions are of the ideal, and in this fact lies the reason for placing them at the top of the hierarchy. If the real progress of man is toward knowledge of ideal truth, it follows that this is an appeal to his highest capacity—his capacity to apprehend what exists absolutely.

The next ranking I offer tentatively, but it seems to me to be relationship or similitude and its subvarieties. I have a consistent impression that the broad resource of analogy, metaphor, and figuration is favored by those of a poetic and imaginative cast of mind. We make use of analogy or comparison when the available knowledge of the subject permits only probable proof. Analogy is reasoning from something we know to something we do not know in one step; hence there is no universal ground for predication. Yet behind every analogy lurks the possibility of a general term. The general term is never established as such, for that would change the argument to one of deductive reasoning with a universal or distributed middle. The user of analogy is hinting at an essence which cannot at the moment be produced. Or, he may be using an indirect approach for reason of tact; analogies not infrequently do lead to generalizations; and he may be employing this approach because he is respectful of his audience and desires them to use their insight.

I mentioned a moment earlier that this type of argument seems to be preferred by those of a poetic or non-literal sort of mind. That fact suggests yet another possibility, which I offer still more diffidently, asking your indulgence if it seems to border on the whimsical. The explanation would be that the cosmos *is* one vast system of analogy, so that our profoundest intuitions of it are made in the form of comparisons. To affirm that something is like something else is to begin to talk about the unitariness of creation. Everything is like everything else somehow, so that we have a ladder of similitude mounting up to the final one-ness—to something like a unity in godhead. Furthermore, there is about this source of argument a kind of decent reticence, a recognition of the unknown along with the known. There is a recognition that the unknown may be continuous with the known, so that man is moving about in a world only partly realized, yet real in all its parts. This is the mood of poetry and mystery, but further adumbration of it I leave to those more gifted than I.

Cause and effect appears in this scale to be a less exalted source of argument, though we all have to use it because we are historical men. Here I must recall the metaphysical ground of this organization and point out that it operates in the realm of becoming. Causes are causes having effect and effects are resulting from causes. To associate this source of argument with its habitual users, I must note that it is heard most commonly from those who are characteristically pragmatic in their way of thinking. It is not unusual today to find a lengthy piece of journalism or an entire political speech which is nothing but a series of arguments from consequence—completely devoid of reference to principle or defined ideas. We rightly recognize these as sensational types of appeal. Those who are partial to arguments based on effect are under a temptation to play too much upon the fears of their audience by stressing the awful nature of some consequence or by exaggerating the power of some cause. Modern advertising is prolific in this kind of abuse. There is likewise a temptation to appeal to prudential considerations only in a passage where things are featured as happening or threatening to happen.

An even less admirable subvariety of this source is the appeal to circumstance, which is the least philosophical of all the topics of argument. Circumstance is an allowable source when we don't know anything else to plead, in which cases we say, "There is nothing else to be done about it." Of all the arguments, it admits of the least perspicaciousness. An example of this which we hear nowadays with great regularity is: "We must adapt ourselves to a fast-changing world." This is pure argument from circumstance. It does not pretend, even, to offer a cause-and-effect explanation. If it did, the first part would tell us why we must adapt ourselves to a fast-changing world; and the second would tell us the result of our doing so. The usually heard formulation does neither. Such argument is preeminently lacking in understanding or what the Greeks called *dianoia*. It simply cites a brute circumstance and says, "Step lively." Actually, this argument amounts to a surrender of reason. Maybe it expresses an instinctive feeling that in this situation reason is powerless. Either you change fast or you get crushed. But surely it would be a counsel of desperation to try only this argument in a world suffering from aimlessness and threatened with destruction.

Generally speaking, cause and effect is a lower-order source of argument because it deals in the realm of the phenomenal, and the phenomenal is easily converted into the sensational. Sensational excitements always run the risk of arousing those excesses which we deplore as sentimentality or brutality.

Arguments based on testimony and authority, utilizing

external sources, have to be judged in a different way. Actually, they are the other sources seen through other eyes. The question of their ranking involves the more general question of the status of authority. Today there is a widespread notion that all authority is presumptuous. ("Authority is authoritarian" seems to be the root idea); consequently it is held improper to try to influence anyone by the prestige of great names or of sanctioned pronouncements. This is a presumption itself, by which every man is presumed to be his own competent judge in all matters. But since that is a manifest impossibility, and is becoming a greater impossibility all the time, as the world piles up bodies of specialized knowledge which no one person can hope to command, arguments based on authority are certainly not going to disappear. The sound maxim is that an argument based on authority is as good as the authority. What we should hope for is a new and discriminating attitude toward what is authoritative, and I would like to see some source recognized as having moral authority. This hope will have to wait upon the recovery of a more stable order of values and the re-recognition of qualities in persons. Speaking most generally, arguments from authority are ethically good when they are deferential toward real hierarchy.

With that we may sum up the rhetorical speaker's obligation toward the ideal, apart from particular determinations. If one accepts the possibility of this or any other ranking, one has to concede that rhetoric is not merely formal; it is realistic. It is not a playing with counters; its impulses come from insights into actuality. Its topic matter is existential, not hypothetical. It involves more than mere demonstration because it involves choice. Its assertions have ontological claims.

Now I return to the second responsibility, which is imposed by the fact that the rhetorician is concerned with definite questions. These are questions having histories, and history is always concrete. This means that the speaker or writer has got to have a rhetorical perception of what his audience needs or will receive or respond to. He takes into account the reality of man's composite being and his tendency to be swayed by sentiment. He estimates the pressures of the particular situation in which his auditors are found. In the eyes of those who look sourly upon the art, he is a man probing for weaknesses which he means to exploit.

But here we must recur to the principle that rhetoric comprehensively considered is an art of emphasis. The definite situation confronts him with a second standard of choice. In view of the receptivity of his audience, which of the topics shall he choose to stress, and how? If he concludes that definition should be the appeal, he tries to express the nature of the thing in a compelling way. If he feels that a cause-and-effect demonstration would stand the greatest chance to impress, he tries to make this linkage so manifest that his hearers will see an inevitability in it. And so on with the other topics, which will be so emphasized or magnified as to produce the response of assent.

Along with this process of amplification, the ancients recognized two qualities of rhetorical discourse which have the effect of impressing an audience with the reality or urgency of a topic. In Greek these appear as *energia* and *enargia*, both of which may be translated "actuality," though the first has to do with liveliness or animation of action and the second with vividness of scene. The speaker now indulges in actualization to make what he is narrating or describing present to the minds' eyes of his hearers.

The practice itself has given rise to a good deal of misunderstanding, which it would be well to remove. We know that one of the conventional criticisms of rhetoric is that the practitioner of it takes advantage of his hearers by playing upon their feelings and imaginations. He over-stresses the importance of his topics by puffing them up, dwelling on them in great detail, using an excess of imagery or of modifiers evoking the senses, and so on. He goes beyond what is fair, the critics often allege, by this actualization of a scene about which the audience ought to be thinking rationally. Since this criticism has a serious basis, I am going to offer an illustration before making the reply. Here is a passage from Daniel Webster's famous speech for the prosecution in the trial of John Francis Knapp. Webster is actualizing for the jury the scene of the murder as he has constructed it from circumstantial evidence.

The deed was executed with a degree of steadiness and self-possession equal to the wickedness with which it was planned. The circumstances now clearly in evidence spread out the scene before us. Deep sleep had fallen upon the destined victim and all beneath his roof. A healthful old man, to whom sleep was sweet, the first sound slumbers of the night held him in their soft but strong embrace. The assassin enters, through a window already prepared, into an unoccupied apartment. With noiseless foot he paces the lonely hall, half-lighted by the moon; he winds up the ascent of the stairs, and reaches the door of the chamber. Of this, he moves the lock by soft and continued pressure, till it turns on its hinges without noise; and he enters, and beholds the victim before him. The room is uncommonly open to the admission of light. The face of the innocent sleeper is turned from the murderer, and the beams of the moon, resting on the gray locks of the aged temple, show him where to strike. The fatal blow is given! and the victim passes, without a struggle or a motion, from the repose of sleep to the repose of death! It is the assassin's purpose to make sure work; and he plies the dagger, though it is obvious that life has been destroyed by the blow of the bludgeon. He even raises the aged arm, that he may not fail in his aim at the heart, and replaces it again over the wound of the poniard! To finish the picture, he explores the wrist for the pulse! He feels for it, and ascertains that it beats no longer! It is accomplished. The deed is done. He retreats, retraces his steps to the window, passes out through it as he came in, and escapes. He has done the murder. No eye has seen him, no ear has heard him. The secret is his own, and it is safe!

By depicting the scene in this fulness of detail, Webster is making it vivid, and "vivid" means "living." There are those who object on general grounds to this sort of dramatization; it is too affecting to the emotions. Beyond a doubt, whenever the rhetorician actualizes an event in this manner, he is making it mean something to the emotional part of us, but that part is involved whenever we are deliberating about goodness and badness. On this subject there is a very wise reminder in Bishop Whately's *Elements of Rhetoric:* "When feelings are strongly excited, they are not necessarily over-excited; it may be that they are only brought to the state which the occasion fully justifies, or even that they fall short of this." Let us think of the situation in which Webster was acting. After all, there is the possibility, or even the likelihood that the murder was committed in this fashion, and that the indicted Knapp deserved the conviction he got. Suppose the audience had remained cold and unmoved. There is the victim's side to consider and the interest of society in protecting life. We should not forget that Webster's "actualization" is in the service of these. Our attitude toward what is just or right or noble and their opposites is not a bloodless calculation, but a feeling for and against. As Whately indicates, the speaker who arouses feeling may only be arousing it to the right pitch and channeling it in the right direction.

To re-affirm the general contention: the rhetorician who

practices "amplification" is not thereby misleading his audience, because we are all men of limited capacity and sensitivity and imagination. We all need to have things pointed out to us, things stressed in our interest. The very task of the rhetorician is to determine what feature of a question is most exigent and to use the power of language to make it appear so. A speaker who dwells insistently upon some aspect of a case may no more be hoodwinking me than a policeman or a doctor when he advises against a certain course of action by pointing out its nature or its consequences. He *should* be in a position to know somewhat better than I do.

It is strongly to be suspected that this charge against rhetoric comes not only from the distorted image that makes man a merely rationalistic being, but also from the dogma of an uncritical equalitarianism. The notion of equality has insinuated itself so far that it appears sometimes as a feeling, to which I would apply the name "sentimental plebeianism," that no man is better or wiser than another, and hence that it is usurpation for one person to undertake to instruct or admonish another. This preposterous (and we could add, wholly unscientific judgment, since our differences are manifold and provable) is propagated in subtle ways by our institutions of publicity and the perverse art of demagogic politics. Common sense replies that any individual who advises a friend or speaks up in meeting is exercising a kind of leadership, which may be justified by superior virtue, knowledge, or personal insight.

The fact that leadership is a human necessity is proof that rhetoric as the attempt through language to make one's point of view prevail grows out of the nature of man. It is not a reflection of any past phase of social development, or any social institution, or any fashion, or any passing vice. When all factors have been considered, it will be seen that men are born rhetoricians, though some are born small ones and others greater, and some cultivate the native gift by study and training, whereas some neglect it. Men are such because they are born into history, with an endowment of passion and a sense of the *ought*. There is ever some discrepancy, however slight, between the situation man is in and the situation he would like to realize. His life is therefore characterized by movement toward goals. It is largely the power of rhetoric which influences and governs that movement.

For the same set of reasons, rhetoric is cognate with language. Ever since I first heard the idea mentioned seriously it impressed me as impossible and even ridiculous that the utterances of men could be neutral. Such study as I have been able to give the subject over the years has confirmed that feeling and has led me to believe that what is sometimes held up as a desideratum—expression purged of all tendency—rests upon an initial misconception of the nature of language.

The condition essential to see is that every use of speech, oral and written, exhibits an attitude, and an attitude implies an act. "Thy speech bewrayeth thee" is aphoristically true if we take it as saying, "Your speech reveals your disposition," first by what you choose to say, then by the amount you decide to say, and so on down through the resources of linguistic elaboration and intonation. All rhetoric is a rhetoric of motives, as Kenneth Burke saw fit to indicate in the title of his book. At the low end of the scale, one may be doing nothing more than making sounds to express exuberance. But if at the other end one sits down to compose a *Critique of the Pure Reason*, one has the motive of refuting other philosophers' account of the constitution of being and of substituting one's own, for an interest which may be universal, but which nonetheless proceeds from the will to alter something.

Does this mean that it is impossible to be objective about anything? Does it mean that one is "rhetorical" in declaring that a straight line is the shortest distance between two points? Not in the sense in which the objection is usually raised. There are degrees of objectivity, and there are various disciplines which have their own rules for expressing their laws or their content in the most effective manner for their purpose. But even this expression can be seen as enclosed in a rhetorical intention. Put in another way, an utterance is capable of rhetorical function and aspect. If one looks widely enough, one can discover its rhetorical dimension, to put it in still another way. The scientist has some interest in setting forth the formulation of some recurrent feature of the physical world, although his own sense of motive may be lost in a general feeling that science is a good thing because it helps progress along.[2]

In short, as long as man is a creature responding to purpose, his linguistic expression will be a carrier of tendency. Where the modern semanticists got off on the wrong foot in their effort to refurbish language lay in the curious supposition that language could and should be outwardly

[2] If I have risked confusion by referring to "rhetoricians" and "rhetorical speakers," and to other men as if they were all non-rhetoricians, while insisting that all language has its rhetorical aspect, let me clarify the terms. By "rhetorician" I mean the deliberate rhetor: the man who understands the nature and aim and requirements of persuasive expression and who uses them more or less consciously according to the approved rules of the art. The other, who by his membership in the family of language users, must be a rhetorician of sorts, is an empirical and adventitious one; he does not know enough to keep invention, arrangement, and style working for him. The rhetorician of my reference is thus the educated speaker; the other is an untaught amateur.

determined. They were positivists operating in the linguistic field. Yet if there is anything that is going to keep on defying positivistic correlation, it is this subjectively born, intimate, and value-laden vehicle which we call language. Language is a system of imputation, by which values and percepts are first framed in the mind and are then imputed to things. This is not an irresponsible imputation; it does not imply, say, that no two people can look at the same clock face and report the same time. The qualities or properties have to be in the things, but they are not in the things in the form in which they are framed by the mind. This much I think we can learn from the great realist-nominalist controversy of the Middle Ages and from the little that contemporary semantics has been able to add to our knowledge. Language was created by the imagination for the purposes of man, but it may have objective reference— just how we cannot say until we are in possession of a more complete metaphysics and epistemology.

Now a system of imputation involves the use of predicates, as when we say, "Sugar is sweet" or "Business is good." Modern positivism and relativism, however, have gone virtually to the point of denying the validity of all conceptual predication. Occasionally at Chicago I purposely needle a class by expressing a general concept in a casual way, whereupon usually I am sternly reminded by some member brought up in the best relativist tradition that "You can't generalize that way." The same view can be encountered in eminent quarters. Justice Oliver Wendell Holmes was fond of saying that the chief end of man is to frame general propositions and that no general proposition is worth a damn. In the first of these general propositions the Justice was right, in the sense that men cannot get along without categorizing their apprehensions of reality.

In the second he was wrong because, although a great jurist, he was not philosopher enough to think the matter through. Positivism and relativism may have rendered a certain service as devil's advocates if they have caused us to be more careful about our concepts and our predicates, yet their position in net form is untenable. The battle against general propositions was lost from the beginning, for just as surely as man is a symbol-using animal (and a symbol transcends the thing symbolized), he is a classifying animal. The morality lies in the application of the predicate.

Language, which is thus predicative, is for the same cause sermonic. We are all of us preachers in private or public capacities. We have no sooner uttered words than we have given impulse to other people to look at the world, or some small part of it, in our way. Thus caught up in a great web of inter-communication and inter-influence, we speak as rhetoricians affecting one another for good or ill. That is why I must agree with Quintilian that the true orator is the good man, skilled in speaking—good in his formed character and right in his ethical philosophy. When to this he adds fertility in invention and skill in the arts of language, he is entitled to that leadership which tradition accords him.

If rhetoric is to be saved from the neglect and even the disrepute which I was deploring at the beginning of this lecture, these primary truths will have to be recovered until they are a part of our active consciousness. They are, in summation, that man is not nor ever can be nor ever should be a depersonalized thinking machine. His feeling is the activity in him most closely related to what used to be called his soul. To appeal to his feeling therefore is not necessarily an insult; it can be a way to honor him, by recognizing him in the fulness of his being. Even in those situations where the appeal is a kind of strategy, it but recognizes that men—all men—are historically conditioned.

Rhetoric must be viewed formally as operating at that point where literature and politics meet, or where literary values and political urgencies can be brought together. The rhetorician makes use of the moving power of literary presentation to induce in his hearers an attitude or decision which is political in the very broadest sense. Perhaps this explains why the successful user of rhetoric is sometimes in bad grace with both camps. For the literary people he is too "practical"; and for the more practical political people he is too "flowery." But there is nothing illegitimate about what he undertakes to do, any more than it would be illegitimate to make use of the timeless principles of aesthetics in the constructing of a public building. Finally, we must never lose sight of the order of values as the ultimate sanction of rhetoric. No one can live a life of direction and purpose without some scheme of values. As rhetoric confronts us with choices involving values, the rhetorician is a preacher to us, noble if he tries to direct our passion toward noble ends and base if he uses our passion to confuse and degrade us. Since all utterance influences us in one or the other of these directions, it is important that the direction be the right one, and it is better if this lay preacher is a master of his art.

Index

Adler, Mortimer, 13, 163
Anderson, Sherwood, 104n
Aristotle, 16, 18–19, 28, 43, 71,
  152–54, 172–73, 176, 205–206,
  208
Arnold, Thurman, 40

Bacon, Sir Francis, 36, 188
Beaton, Kendall, 8n
Burke, Edmund, 14n, 25, 26, 106,
  135, 202
Burke, Kenneth, 16, 27, 78, 103,
  138, 152, 221
Byron, Lord, 98

Chase, Stuart, 63
Churchill, Winston, 76–77, 161
Cicero, 16, 208
Communication, and cognition,
  121
Corbett, Edward P. J., 28–29
Cratylus, 117, 193. *See also* Plato
Croce, Benedetto, 122

Davidson, Donald, 8n, 10
Definition: argument from, 209–
  13; stipulative, 213
Definiendum, 43

Dehmlow, Louis, 8n
Dialectic: defined, 19, 54, 144–48,
  162–63; function of, 71, 73–74;
  and history, 182; limitations of,
  174–75; and logic, 173–74, 197;
  method of, 169; and probability,
  19; and rhetoric, 32, 71, 77–78,
  138, 160, 162–84; role of, 162–84
  passim; and science, 164; and social cohesion, 175, 181; and social
  scientist, 138. *See also* Rhetoric
Dialectician, 78, 157, 163–64, 175,
  197. *See also* Dialectic
Duhamel, P. Albert, 58n

Ebbitt, Wilma, 6, 16n
Eliot, T. S., 3, 48, 96
Emerson, Ralph Waldo, 33
Enargia, 217
Energia, 217

Foreign language: value of study of,
  53

"GI rhetoric," 103–104

Hayakawa, S. I., 11–12, 32, 38
Hayek, F. A., 143

227

Hemingway, Ernest, 104
Heraclitus, 36
Hinton, Norman, 41
Hobbes, Thomas, 35–36
Hobbs, A. H., 151
Holmes, Oliver Wendell, Jr., 119,
  223–24
Huxley, T. H., 63n, 204

Ideographs, 126
Ideology: defined, 133

James, Henry, 96
Journalism: study of, 53

Kendall, Willmoore, 9, 10
Kirk, Russell, 5, 9, 12, 26
Korzybski, Alfred, 36, 42

Language: abstracting in, 41; as
"covenant," 136; and behaviorism,
43n; conventionalizing property
of, 127; defined, 120–21, 223; defining and ordering function of,
54–55; and definition, 40, 41,
54–55; and dialectic, 162; duty
of, 178; and epistemology, 40;
evocative power of, 45, 52–53;
and "god terms," 85; and intuition, 43; in journalism, 67; in
judicial process, 54–55; and meaning, 44–46; mathematical, 208n;
and memory, 44; and metaphor,
52; metaphysical community of,
51; movement by, 60–61; and
myth, 34–35; "neuter," 64; and
order, 34, 54–55; poetical quality
of, 51; philosophical quality
of, 35–37; prescriptive meaning,
135; and preservation of cultural
tradition, 129; restoration of,
45–55; sermonic nature of, 181,
224–25; of social property, 191;
suprapersonal nature of, 35; symbolic nature of, 45–47; as system
of forms, 38–39; as system of imputation, 223; synthesizing power

of, 45; teachers of, as philosophers,
196; and tendency, 37, 73, 79,
221; theories of origin of, 119–20;
transcendental basis of, 133; and
values, 38–40, 48, 51, 197, 223.
See also Dialectic, Rhetoric
Lawgivers: as definers, 54
Lincoln, Abraham, 22–23, 25n, 26
"Linguistic drift," 130
Locke, John, 121
Lundberg, George, 153

MacArthur, Douglas, 47, 161
Mailer, Norman, 104
Maritain, Jacques, 78, 81
Milton, John, 20n, 115
Modern Age, 9

Naming, 34–35, 117–18, 121, 124,
  144, 174–75, 192–93, 197. See
also Language
National Review, 9
Neumeyer, Martin, 153
Niebuhr, Reinhold, 3
Nietzsche, Friedrich, 165, 177

Occam, William, 36
Opinion: and cultural cohesion,
  182–83
Orwell, George, 107, 109

Péguy, Charles, 48
Pericles, 170
Persuasion: as "psychological coercion," 178
Phaedrus, 57–83 passim; 169–71.
See also Plato
Plato, 11–12, 16, 43, 47, 54, 57–83
passsim, 117, 163–84 passim, 193,
196; as "master rhetorician," 75;
as rhetorician, 171; rhetoric of,
182
Poetry: poet's role in society, 48;
discipline of, 52–53; and language,
48–52; function of, 70; and values,
51–55, 169–70

Quintilian, 16, 208, 224

Ransom, John Crowe, 4, 10
Recte loqui, 188, 190–91
Relativism, 116–36 passim, 195, 223–24
Rhetoric: as actualization, 18, 77, 217–21; advisory nature of, 17–18, 220; and amplification, 217–21; analogical nature of, 80, 141, 169, 213–14; argument from authority in, 27, 150–52, 215–17; argument from circumstance in, 24–27, 215; argument from definition in, 21–23, 213–15; argument from similitude in, 22–23, 141, 209, 214–15; as an art, 171; as art of persuasion, 140–41; and axiology, 17–18, 56, 60, 72, 76, 80–83, 140–41, 183–84; base, 66; cause and effect argument in, 141, 209, 214–15; cognate with language, 220–21; conceived as artifice, 58; contrasted with symbolic logic, 207–208; and "cultural cohesion," 4, 138; and decline of Christianity, 177–78; and decline of Western culture, 177–78; defined, 16–17, 56, 144, 162, 207–208, 211–12, 217, 220, 225; deliberative, 152–55; and democracy, 85; and dialectic, 18–19, 32, 51, 71–74, 77, 81, 138, 162–84; emotional appeals in, 205; enthymeme and use of, 28, 154–56, 172–75; epideictic, 152; as form of eros, 83; ethics and, 86; example in, 172; and "excluded middle," 22n, 54; figuration in, 58, 213–14; forensic, 152; "formal rhetoric," 208; function of, 17–18, 70, 76, 80, 82, 85, 171, 172, 182, 205–206, 220; and "the Good," 74, 80–81; and history, 32, 161–63, 171–72, 181–84, 206–207, 217, 224–25; and the human condition, 203–204, 207; as a humanistic discipline, 184, 201, 206; conceived as idea, 58; and identification, 16, 138, 143–44, 154; and literary values, 225; and literature, 51, 207, 225; and logic, 203–11; and memory, 161–83; and modes of apprehension, 13–14; and "movement of the soul," 73, 80, 82; and movement toward goals, 140–42, 171–72, 206, 221, 224; and myth, 153; noble, 68–74, 158; object of, 19–20; "office" of, 171–73, 211–12; and ontological referents, 188; and the "order of the goods," 66, 80, 85, 211; and persuasion, 205–206, 211; and philosophy, 188; poetical resources of, 51; and policy, 56; and politics, 212, 225; power of, 80, 188; prejudice against, 161, 177–78, 201, 206; and probability, 19; and propaganda, 80–81, 183; and prophecy, 76; questions susceptible to treatment by, 161–62, 217; and "real world," 207–208; Renaissance manuals of, 188; restoration of, 224–25; role of, 3–6, 8, 78, 206–12; of scene, 148; and science, 141–42, 157, 203–206; and scientific data, 148–49; and "sense of the ought," 221; sentimental, 52; and social science, 140; and style, 20, 28, 64; as substantive discipline, 201, 211–12, 224–25; teachers of, 202–203; and terms, 22–23, 80, 111; and topics, 21, 28, 173–74; and tragedy, 79n, 177n; and truth, 71, 213; and values, 4, 13, 16, 20, 29, 80–83, 89, 105, 111, 139, 141–45, 155–58, 180–83, 211–12, 216–17, 221–25; as "vehicle of order," 34
Rhetorical education, 51, 188–98 passim
"Rhetorical induction." See Rhetoric, example
Rhetorical language, 63–65
Rhetorical maneuver, 143–44

"Rhetorical prevarication," 133
Rhetorical syllogism. *See* Rhetoric, enthymeme
Rhetorical terms, 80
Rhetorician: the base, 66; the complete, 141; definition of, 222n; the evil, 111; the honest, 144, 211; the noble, 18, 74–78; responsibility of the, 60, 211, 216; the true, 74–75; the virtuous, 73
Robinson, Rev. John, 47

Santayana, George, 195
Sapir, Edward, 120, 130
Science, 203–204
Semantic change, 129, 131, 133
"Semantic shift," 130
Semantics, 36–46, 62, 116, 160–61, 178–80, 184, 197, 222–24. *See also* Language
Shelley, Percy Bysshe, 44, 48, 122
Signs: conventional, 125
Social scientists, 139–58 *passim*
Socrates, 41, 53, 57–83 *passim*, 164–71 *passim*, 175–80 *passim*, 182–83
Socratic dialogue: characterized, 58–59
Sociologists, 138–59 *passim*
Spinoza, Baruch, 81
Symbolic logic, 207–208

Tate, Allen, 10
Taylor, A. E., 58n
Teachers: as definers, 50, 187–98; as upholders of established institutions, 191
Terms: acronyms, 108–109; cause and, 209; charismatic, 86, 109–10; cultural change and, 97; defined, 87–88; "devil," 100; dialectical, 72, 144–48; ethical use of, 111–12; examples of ultimate, 90, 92, 94–96, 98, 101–102, 107, 111, 157, 194; and evaluation, 146–47; "god," 88; hypostatized, 92; inverted, 103–106; melioristic bias in, 151; myth and, 153; naming and, 87–88; persuasion and, 112; politicians' use of, 107; positive, 72, 138, 144–48; of repulsion, 99, 100; secondary, 110; and "tendency," 142; ultimate, 86, 109–12 *passim*; uncontested, 101, 102; undefined, 42; and values, 89, 94, 105, 111

Thucydides, 49
Tillieh, Paul, 7
Topics, 208–18 *passim*

Urban, Wilbur Marshall, 44–45, 121
Utiliter loqui, 189

Values. *See* Rhetoric
Vere loqui, 188–89, 191
Vinson, Fred M., 119
Vivas, Eliseo, 7
Vossler, Karl, 35

Warren, Robert Penn, 10
Weaver, Richard M.: Agrarian ideals of, 10–11; biographical data on, 3–6, 7n, 8, 11; as conservative, 8, 12, 15; and defense of orthodoxy, 4–5; as "doctor of culture," 4–5; influence of, 28–29; major publications of, 8–9; philosophy of, 9–15; as political conservative, 8–12; southern influences on, 4–5; influence of Plato on, 11–30 *passim*
Webster, Daniel, 218–19
Whatley, Richard, 219
Whorf, Benjamin Lee, 127
Words: analogizing function of, 129; power of, 33–56 *passim*, 188; power of, to define, 37. *See also* Language

Young Americans for Freedom, 10
Yeats, William Butler, 48